FORTUNE TELLING BY JAPANESE SWORDS

FORTUNE TELLING BY JAPANESE SWORDS

FROM AM OLD MANUSCRIPT

BY

O'HAMAGUCHI

AND

TALBOT CLIFTON, F.R.G.S.

with an Introduction and Notes by

Daniel Bürgin

Klaus ISELE Editor

Cover: Oshigata of the »Horio-Chōgi« blade;
the favourite katana of the third Horio Daimyō of Matsue

www.klausisele.de

Publisher: BoD · Books on Demand GmbH,
Überseering 33, 22297 Hamburg, bod@bod.de
Print: Libri Plureos GmbH,
Friedensallee 273, 22763 Hamburg
ISBN: 978-3-8423-6136-2

DANIEL BÜRGIN

About "Fortune Telling with Japanese Swords" and the Tradition of *Kensō* 剣相

The tradition of *kensō* 剣相

In Japan, divining the future with swords is called *kensō* 剣相. It has a long tradition, although limited literature in English is available

According to Markus Sesko ("Legends and Stories around the Japanese Sword", Vol. 2, Lulu Enterprise, Inc., 2012), *kensō* is much older than the tradition of sword appraisals, and the earliest written note in Japan dates from 1423. In the Muromachi Period (1392-1573), it was advised to carve the Sanskrit character bhrūṃ (Japanese: boron) around the signature in the case of cursed swords. This character drives out evil and is a purifying symbol.

Further, Sesko explains that the origins of systematic *kensō* rituals come from Kyūshū's Bungo Province in the Muromachi Period. It became fully established in Japan in the middle of the Edo Period (1600-1867). Publications increased from the middle of the 19th century, with nine different schools evolving and competing against each other. *Kensō* was performed following the opposing principles of ying and yang, which are interconnected and interdependent.

Sesko also gives practical examples that resonate with Clifton's book on 'Fortune Telling by Japanese Swords":

"If sun or crescent shaped tobiyaki (飛焼き) – small isolated temper elements atop of the actual temper line (*hamon*, 刃文) – were spotted, the *kensō* would say that this was a very auspicious omen. But slanting *saka-ashi* (逆足) counteract their power, that means they lower the auspicious effect of the *tobiyaki*. Regular *ashi* on the other hand, that means *ashi* which form a *midare-hamon* (乱れ刃文) with a regular rhythm, stood for luck and a secure, harmonious married life."

During the mid-Edo Period, *kensō* was en vogue and influential to the point that it became irrational. Sword smiths focused on making blades that were of good omen. Some samurai had their old valuable blades reworked and shortened to a length considered lucky to avoid misfortune. For example, in the Yanagawa castle in Chikugo province, the Tachibana *daimyō's*, a feudal lord's, younger brother, Tachibana Naotsugu, avoided using blades that had records of a bad *kensō*. Overall, negative signs in a blade counted for larger numbers than good omens. Clifton's book confirms this statement. He lists forty-one lucky fortunes versus one hundred and four negative ones. Most blades must have foretold a perilous future for their owners.

Kensō became so absurd that when, in 1830, a *daimyō* gathered his high-ranking retainers for a New Year's banquet and invited a *kensō* expert who was to appraise the swords of two retainers present, emotions escalated. One had a blade of the smith Shimozaka of Echizen province. "Shimozaka", meaning downhill, was considered a bad omen. The other samurai had a sword with a *gyaku chōji midare* (reversed irregular clove pattern) in the *hamon* that was slanting towards the tang, signifying defiance of one's lord. The two samurai owning these blades were so furious about the negative interpretation by the *kensō* expert that they visited him the following day and challenged him to a fight. He was so terrified by the prospect of a deadly duel that he asked for forgiveness. To settle the issue, the expert had to write a letter to the two samurai comitting to immediately cease practicing *kensō*. Satisfied with the letter, the two samurai left. This widely known incident motivated *kensō* professionals to offer only positive interpretations. Consequently, around 1861, fewer and fewer samurai became interested in fortune-telling by swords, and the practice started to disappear.

John Talbot Clifton discovered *kensō* when it had already been in decline for several decades.

*

About this "Fortune Telling by Japanese Swords" and some interpretations from the divinations in Clifton's book

I discovered this small volume of "Fortune Telling by Japanese Swords" in a second-hand bookstore a few years ago. It was issued in 1905 as a private edition by the English traveler John Talbot Clifton (1868-1928). At the time, I bought the book out of curiosity as an addition to other Japanese sword-related books.

Recently, I pulled "Fortune Telling by Japanese Swords" off the shelf and began to study its peculiar text and drawings in more detail for the first time. Looking at the simple drawings, which obviously showed common faults as well as planned activities of steel patterns in a blade, my interest in the book grew as I became curious to learn more about its publisher.

Talbot Clifton had prepared a summary of *kensō*, the tradition of divining the future based on appearances and faults in a Japanese sword. It was a topic I had heard of, but had never bothered to learn more about until now.

Spending time with Clifton's book, I realised that many of the divinations were based on either technical faults, i.e., *ware*, general cracks and openings in Japanese blades, *hada ware*, cracks in the steel surface of the blade created by a swordsmith's lack of skill, or on desirable metallurgical activities, occurring during the process of making a katana. These desirable traits are produced during the quenching process when the cutting edge of a blade is being hardened. In simplified terms, the forged blade is coated with an adhesive clay mixture (clay, charcoal powder, pulverized sandstone). This mixture is applied to the blade with a spatula and is scraped off to a very thin layer, where the *hamon* will be. The composition of the clay mixture varies between schools and individual smiths. Once dry, the coated blade will be reheated and quenched in cold water. The shock of the rapidly cooling steel triggers a chemical reaction, and martensite structures occur. The coating prevents the blade from cooling too fast and hardening. It will also create the sharp outline of the cutting edge, the *hamon*, where the steel cools more rapidly due to the coating being a thin layer.

After polishing a blade, the martensite structures become visible on the surface of the steel. Their various formations and shapes were given specific, often poetic, names. They form an integral part of appreciating the beauty of a Japanese sword. Their appearance and formations also help identify specific characteristics, such as age, origin (in terms of sword-smithing tradition, school), and maker of a sword.

In other words, divinations of good and bad fortunes were based on structural faults and desired metallurgical activities.

Was there a link between bad and good luck prophecies and their underlying nature deriving from either a fault or desired activity?

The sketches in Talbot Clifton's book visualize the difference between flaws and activities. Was he aware of their differences, or did he inherit the drawings and the comments without further knowledge? – Who knows; but looking at the sketches in his book, *ware*, flaws are drawn as solid black lines, dots, and patches, whilst *hataraki*, metallurgical activities, are mostly represented with dotted or thinner, less intense lines. Studying the drawings, it becomes evident in most cases what represents cracks in a blade and what usually represents martensitic activities, i.e., the appearance of *nie* or *nioi* formations. Both are clusters of martensite with the difference that for *nie*, the observer can see the individual sparkling martensite crystal with the eye, while *nioi* are too small to be distinguished individually.

Hence, it makes logical sense that divinations based on *ware*, flaws, represent variations of bad luck. Conversely, desired activities in a blade produced during the forging process stand for lucky omens. However, this is not an absolute rule. The position of a martensitic structure on the blade, such as one resembling a dragon, can turn a prediction of good luck into ill luck if, for example, the imagined dragon's head faces towards the *nakago*, the tang, of the blade instead of the *kissaki*, the tip.

For example, Plate XL.'s Figure 1. shows a crack inside the *bōshi*, the hardened cutting edge in the blade's *kissaki*. It is a fatal flaw, as the tip would be at risk of breaking during a fight. Accordingly, Clifton states that Figure 1. has "a very bad meaning, albeit very difficult to explain". The same Plate XL. has two more divinations (Figures 2. and 3.). Figure 2. shows three round clusters of what appear to be desired *nie*, martensite structures on the surface of the steel, also called *tobiyaki*, "flying hardened spots" detached from the *hamon*, the hardened cutting edge. In the book, Figure 2. is considered "an excellent sign of good fortunes". Having the spots occur so neatly arranged, as shown in the diagram, would be a rare appearance in a blade. It makes logical sense to interpret it as a sign of good fortune. Similarly, Figure 3. in Plate XL. stands for good fortune as well, showing a metallurgical activity interpreted as the shape of an animal with its head pointing towards the *kissaki*. The line drawn in the diagram for Figure 2. is more ambiguous than for Figure 1. and Figure 3. I still believe it represents a structural activity in the steel and not a fault as shown in Figure 1., where the line of the sketch is thick and intensely black.

A second example of an inferior-quality blade is Plate XXI. The temper line of the *bōshi* fades out before reaching the point and before running into the back of the blade. In this diagram, the smith failed to harden the sword's tip entirely when quenching, and its strength is suboptimal. It is unsurprising that this diagram also signifies bad luck.

A third example is Plate XVII. Here, the drawings are of dotted circles and a dotted sickle moon-shape in the *jihada*, which is the visible surface of the blade's steel. All these drawings are lucky omens and look very much like clusters of *nie*, shiny particles of martensite. The positive interpretations make sense from a technical perspective, just as the imperfectly forged blade in Plate XXI. can be expected to bring bad luck to the owner.

Whilst these examples follow the logic of what makes a strong or a weak katana, other drawings and interpretations sometimes feel more arbitrary.

About the author and his source

John Talbot Clifton (1868-1928), commonly known as Talbot Clifton, was an extensive traveler and adventurer who visited Japan, likely in the first years of the early twentieth century. Unfortunately, no explicit dates are available for when exactly and how long he spent time there, adding a sense of mystery to what he did and experienced in Japan.

In "The Book of Talbot", published in 1933 by his widow, Mary Violet Clifton, commonly known as Violet Clifton, she mentions that Talbot covered the Sino-Russian War, which lasted from 1904 to 1905. This information suggests that he might have set foot in Japan during this period. His book, "Fortune Telling with Japanese Swords", was published in 1905 when the conflict ended. Unfortunately, Violet Clifton's biography of her late husband does not delve into his travels in Japan.

Talbot Clifton writes in the preface to his book that "while wandering Japan, I happened to come across two or three books on Fortune-Telling by Swords". He explains that his goal in publishing the book was to gain a wider audience's interest in Japanese swords. Clifton himself brought numerous katanas back to England. He was fond of Japanese swords and their special status, as well as the spiritual connection with a blade, enjoyed by the Japanese. Violet writes only briefly about Talbot's stay in Japan and his fondness for katana and other things

Japanese. Talbot had brought back not only swords but also Japanese Buddhist bronze sculptures, kimonos, and "Satsuma China" (the porcelain of the Satsuma kilns from Kyūshū that are still highly valued today). Violet's short paragraph related to things Japanese describes how her husband taught her about *ikebana*, the Japanese flower arrangement. He explained to her that "arranging flowers is like singing a song or writing a lyric".

When it comes to katana, Violet writes:

"Out of a sheath of silk, out of scabbard of wood, Talbot would draw a sword of the samurai. He had many such. He told Violet that these swords guarded a special darling-honour known only to the nobles of Japan. Unsheathing a sword, Talbot would bow, and turn his head so that his breath would not sully the blade. He said: I was taught to do that in Japan. Such swords as these were made by men, honoured throughout the ages; they were forged with fasting and with prayer, and into its owner was said to enter the spirit of the sword. Men, skilled in reading the blades of swords, would see in a flaw in the steel, in a waving line, or in a mark, the symbol of bird, of sky or of beast. By that means was foretold fortune or disaster to those who owned the weapon."

From this description, it is evident that Talbot Clifton was not just fond of *nihontō*, Japanese blades, as an art object and weapon, but was taught about them culturally whilst in Japan. From Violet's description it is clear that he properly stored their *shirasaya*, their plain wooden scabbards, in a silk bag, as is still the custom today. He avoided having his breath hit the steel, knowing this could easily result in stains and rust if not removed immediately. Clifton referred Violet to the adage "the sword is the soul of the samurai", a quote attributed to Tokugawa Ieyasu, the first Tokugawa shōgun. Clifton also knew that Japanese swordsmiths had their forges sanctified as a Shintō shrine.

Violet's "Book of Talbot" also briefly mentions the "emperor of Japan, who gave up his throne so that he might have more leisure for this joy." Rather than the emperor of Japan, the passage refers to the last Tokugawa shōgun, Yoshinobu, who abdicated in 1867 and enjoyed his life as a private citizen into the early twentieth century, with photography becoming his passion and hobby. At the time, it was common for Western visitors to mistake the shōgun as the emperor, as he had yielded the true power in the country until Yoshinobu's abdication in November 1867. For most of Japan's history over the previous eight hundred years, the emperor and the aristocracy were secluded in Kyōto without any real power, which was held by the warrior class, the shōgun, and his samurai class.

Reading Violet Clifton's description shows that her late husband had developed a genuine passion for *nihontō* during his visit to Japan. Japanese swords must have appealed to Clifton as an adventurer and an English aristocrat. His declared intent to rouse more interest in

Japanese swords by publishing his book, "Fortune Telling with Japanese Swords", feels genuine.

*

Who was the person who introduced Clifton to *kensō*? Who translated the text – for the original books surely were in Japanese – and who did the simple drawings?

On the book's title page, Clifton mentions his source, which he acknowledges as a certain O'Hamaguchi and an old manuscript. We can assume that Clifton obtained the manuscript from O'Hamaguchi. However, any search for O'Hamaguchi's identity has been fruitless so far. I could not trace him in either Japanese or non-Japanese literature. As for the drawings, it is possible that Clifton drew them himself from the original source or asked someone to copy them.

In his 1905 published book, Talbot Clifton also dedicated with his "sincerest affections" the privately circulated manuscript to "Sir James Drummond, Bart.", who can be identified as Sir James Hamlyn Williams, the fifth Baronet Forbes-Drummond (1891-1970). He was Talbot Clifton's much younger half-brother. They shared the same mother, Madeline-Diana Elizabeth (Agnew) Williams Drummond, who remarried after the death of Talbot's father when he was still a child.

Like his half-brother, John Talbot Clifton came from an old family. The Cliftons were the ancestral owners of one of Lancashire's largest and most prestigious agricultural estates. At the age of fourteen, Talbot became the heir to the Clifton Estate of Lytham Hall after his grandfather passed away.

Talbot Clifton was educated at Eton and Cambridge. In the way Violet Clifton vaguely writes about his education in her "The Book of Talbot", he might not have completed his studies or left immediately after graduation on a schooner for Australia that would have taken him eighty days.

According to her, Talbot had:

"...already travelled before he was twenty round the world twice, choosing adventure rather than the enjoyment of the ancient vast estates in the Fylde, which wealth had come to him when his grandfather died. Talbot was then but sixteen years of age; his father had died when he was a child."

We get the sense of an adventurer exploring the world's last frontiers, risking his life in multiple situations. Despite his adventurous spirit, Clifton never traveled without his Shakespeare, pen and pencils, keeping fragmented diaries and sketching landscapes.

These diary fragments would become the source of Violet Clifton's biography for the time before their marriage and joint travels. To put it in Talbot Clifton's own words while he was in maddening pain as he recovered from an abscess on his chest on one of his trips:

"Did nothing all day. Lay on my back. Learnt Spanish, sketched and Shakespeare. (...) Very ill, wrote thirty pages of my novel." And again: "Chest aching. Sat up all night writing poems like a demon a-blood-curdling; these relieve my mind."

Clifton's traveling was compulsive, and he covered all five continents at a time when it was never certain one would return home alive. Despite his physical strength, he regularly fell seriously ill when exploring the world. Still, he recovered each time until his last trip in 1928.

Being a child of his time and given his social status, Talbot was an avid hunter. He shot animals during his travels, both for leisure and sometimes for survival. In one anecdote, Clifton even ate from a frozen mammoth preserved in the Arctic permafrost. As a hunter in the late nineteenth century, he was shooting undiscovered species that would end up being named after him (E.g., Clifton's bighorn, a Siberian sheep).

"His travels were his means of asceticism and escape", concluded Violet.

When traveling in Peru, John Talbot Clifton encountered a soulmate when he met Mary Violet Beauclerk (1883-1961), a writer. Mary Violet's pedigree matched Clifton's. She was a descendent of Charles Beauclerk, the first Duke of St. Albans and the illegitimate son of King Charles II. Violet's father, working in the diplomatic service, had taken her to Peru. She had not lived in England since childhood, and had not the traditional education of a woman of her time. From a young age, she was very strong-willed and embraced a destiny that did not conform to society's expectations for women. Violet writes of herself as an adolescent: "I shall be the wife of an officer and follow him in wars." She would creep out of bed and sleep on the floor to become hardy.

In this spirit, the young Violet invented a game she called "The Game of Bearing". A boy would whip the legs of Violet and her friends, who stood in a line. Whoever jumped away lost, and the one who resisted the pain the longest won. Violet does not comment on whether her friends willingly joined this spartan-like game. I would be surprised if it was their favourite, but they probably had to yield to Violet's pressure. She does not say who the winner was, but it is likely her. "Your body must be the slave of your will", she wrote as a teenager. Violet felt her destiny so strongly that later, when she fell in love with a man who courted her and spoke of marriage, Violet was compelled to answer: "I could marry you, but yet I am afraid because I think that somewhere there is a man I was born to follow; when I meet him I shall be certain that he is my lodestar." – John Talbot Clifton would be that man.

Somewhat unusually for England's high society at the time, it was not an arranged wedding, but a love marriage. Talbot confessed his feelings in the town of Miraflores, Peru. As a first present, he gave Violet the volume of Shakespeare he had traveled with and poetically inscribed it *To the Only One in the Wanderings of a Wanderer*. Violet would keep the book until the end of her life. Yet, after his death, she never wore his family's jewels again, which he had presented to her when she became his wife. – A source (not Violet, however) wrote that Talbot fell in love with the much younger woman after he heard that Violet had shot her horse because she couldn't bear the thought of anyone else riding it. It was a cruel deed, and undoubtedly extreme even for her time, particularly with a woman pulling the trigger. Her willpower and steeliness must have attracted the adventurer. Surely, Violet must have felt for that poor horse she killed. Nonetheless, she displayed a fierce, arrogant attitude towards owning the animal she did not want to share with anyone. For her, that ownership extended to the horse's life. This story rings true, as befits the picture of the adolescent she described in "The Book of Talbot". While Violet demonstrated traits one might deem despicable today, Talbot judged them differently: it was about strength of mind over emotion and body, a motif that regularly appears in her book.

The couple married in London in 1907. Talbot Clifton was thirty-nine, and Mary Violet was twenty-four. Both genuinely enjoyed the sense of adventure of traveling to many faraway places together. He saw his wife as an equal. Talbot would proactively invite Violet to his adventurous travels after marriage, as when he traveled to Baghdad, for example. These were offers that Violet would accept without hesitation, and sometimes she would even ask to join. In 1917, during World War I., Violet learned that her husband got an order to search for submarines around the coast. Upon learning of his task, she left him a note: "How gay to die with Talbot, how drab to live without him." It was a request to which he replied: "Be quick then, I am going on this tide."

In "The Book of Talbot", Violet critically assesses their marriage, including interpersonal difficulties they faced as a couple and eventually overcame. Ultimately, their love and mutual respect rose above any challenges they had faced during their relationship.

In 1928, the Cliftons traveled together to Timbuktu but were forced to abort the voyage in Mali as Talbot became ill, suffering from late-stage lung cancer. Timbuktu was a place Clifton had been keen to visit, and it is possible that the eccentric adventurer sensed or even knew that he would not survive this last journey.

Talbot Clifton passed away on their return to England when stopping over in the Canary Islands. Violet had his body embalmed and brought it back home for burial. Out of superstition, no ship wanted a coffin as a cargo. It was only because of Violet's determination and mental fortitude that she eventually found a small Norwegian vessel trading in fruit willing to take her and the coffin back to London.

Five years later, Mary Violet published "The Book of Talbot", a biography of her late husband based on his fragmented travel diaries and their joint travels. With this book, Mary Violet Clifton won the English James Tait Black Prize for literature in 1933, and two years later, she was nominated for the Nobel Prize in Literature, though she did not win.

Talbot Clifton's biography and other books of her such as "Visions of Peru" are still in print and interesting to read. Clifton's biography provides insights into their lives and personalities, and Talbot's courage that was close to recklessness, and describes his many adventures, from washing gold in Alaska's Yukon River and the Antarctic Region to journeys in Africa, the Middle East, Myanmar, and Tibet.

Mary Violet and John Talbot Clifton must have made a unique couple in their lifetime. Talbot was the heir to a large estate, and both had famous ancestors. Talbot Clifton seems to have been more of a maverick, adventurer, and philosopher than an English landlord, and Violet shared his tastes. He must have been the incarnation of her childhood dreams of a husband, the man she had hardened herself and waited for. Although a fearless adventurer, Talbot was also politically active, serving as a Justice of Peace in Lancashire. His track record with finances was more dubious. He was quoted as a thoughtless spendthrift and showed limited interest in the affairs of his hereditary Lytham estate, which, after his death would eventually descend into ruin.

Mary Violet, the successful writer, complements his picture. They were a couple who mutually respected and admired one other, and shared a passion for travel and taste for adventure. During their years in England (one is tempted to write "in between their travels"), Violet gave birth to three daughters and two sons. Violet writes that her children must have felt neglected, for she "would not weigh them against her husband and would, at any time, leave them to follow him". Although they were parents, the couple lived a life that often took place very much outside the typical lifestyle and societal norms and obligations expected of England's high society. Despite their illustrious ancestry, Talbot and Violet come across as individuals who are adamant about defining themselves rather than being defined by society.

Concluding her "Book of Talbot", Mary Violet chose pictures of her and her husband, which are inserted below. His is a painting showing Talbot gazing with bright eyes into the distance. Clifton is dressed in a thick fur coat befitting an Arctic explorer. We encounter an adventurer and hero, not a landlord. Clifton shows no interest either in the painter or those who will admire his picture. His interests, he seems to say with this portrait, lie elsewhere. His eyes have a philosophical expression, simultaneously curious and knowing what happens beyond the moment of his posing. Violet's picture is blurry, with the camera focusing on her eyes. It is the opposite of her husband's. We look straight into a woman's piercing, intelligent eyes asserting her independence and challenging the viewer.

The two pictures leave an impression that is more reminiscent of a twentieth-century hippie couple than the landlord and landlady of a great English estate.

*

Unfortunately, in the context of Talbot Clifton's book "Fortune Telling with Japanese Swords", Clifton's trip to Japan did not make it into Violet's biography for whatever reasons. However, one paragraph I have quoted above mentions Talbot's admiration for *nihontō*, Japanese blades. It would have been interesting to learn more about how Clifton got interested in *kensō* and to read about his adventures and experiences in a Japan that had recently and rather abruptly emerged from a feudal system after close to three hundred years of isolation. After all, Talbot Clifton was in Japan at a time of tremendous cultural change when Western visitors were few.

*

This 2025 reprint of Clifton's "Fortune Telling with Japanese Swords" remains in line with the author's original intention: "To make more people interested in swords, Japanese or otherwise than is at present the case; for a lover of swords and sword-handles is a matter of great interest to many in Japan."

John Talbot Clifton

Mary Violet Clifton

PREFACE

WHILE wandering in Japan I happened to come across two or three books on Fortunetelling by Swords, which I believe are now out of print. The object of translating a book of this kind into English is to make more people interested in swords, Japanese or otherwise, than is at present the case; for a lover of swords and sword-handles is a matter of great interest to many in Japan; at the same time I should say that many judges take more interest in these curious markings than they would like to admit. Now take the uninitiated; they may have heard that So-and-so possesses a collection of swords, and the usual question is what good are they, and what an uninteresting hobby. Now let them know that fortunes can be told by them and you will at once arouse their curiosity, which probably will only be appeased when they have seen the swords for themselves, which in a few cases I hope will be instrumental in their taking a further interest in blades. To understand that the ancient sword of Japan was not manufactured, but was made by the spirit; that the great sword-makers have been from the year 900 A.D. almost up to the present date honoured by the highest people in the land; that the spirit of the sword when held is supposed to impart itself to the holder; while on its clear surface can be seen Nature in almost all its beauties, such as rivers, forests, and lakes, waves, and sky, birds, and beast. A volume dealing far more deeply into the mystery of this interesting weapon I hope to have shortly ready.

TALBOT CLIFTON (1905)

PLATE I.

Swords are divided into five parts, by which fortunes can be told, viz.:

> san – *dispersing*
>
> Fuku – *luck*
>
> Shū – *accumulation*
>
> mei – *life*
>
> Un – *destiny*

Figure 1. – San means to disperse or scatter, either for good or evil.

Figure 2. – Shū means an accumulation of things, either good or bad, in regard to fortune.

Figure 3. – Fuku means either good or bad luck.

Figure 4 – Mei means a long or short life.

Figure 5. – Un means destiny.

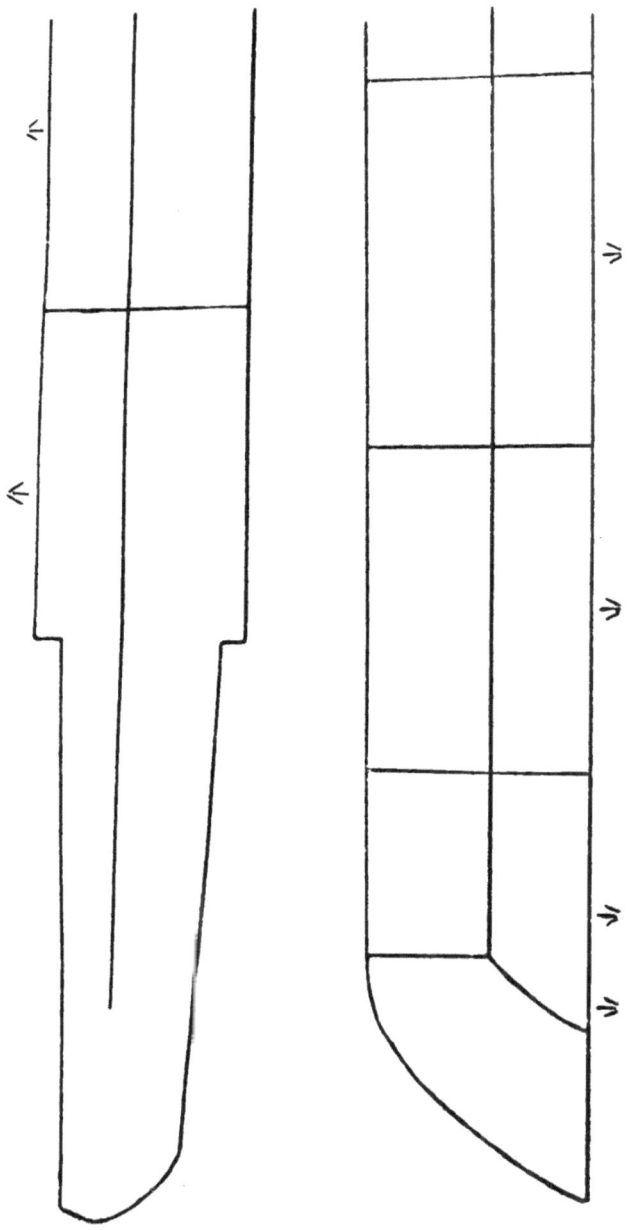

PLATE II.

Mekugi-ana, or hole, is found on the hilt of every sword: sometimes there being two, sometimes three.

Gyakuryū means a dragon upside down.

Hamon is the Japanese for the temper of the sword.

Figure 1 means that if a man possesses a sword with a mark like this, and he falls ill, he will never recover.

Figure 2. – Something is bound to happen for the man; he will either lose his property, or there will be illness in his house.

Figure 3. – A dragon upside down is a sign that every battle the possessor fights he will lose. It would be better luck if the dragon was facing the opposite direction.

Figure 4. – As this mark is not in the shape of an opal, it is unlucky.

Figure 5, as a rule, is very hard to see; it means quarrelling with people above you, or with one>s parents.

Figure 6. – This hole, if it is too far up at the end, ought to be filled, as it shows a low social position, an unsettled home, and, if it belonged to any great General, it would mean misfortunes, defeats, and general misery.

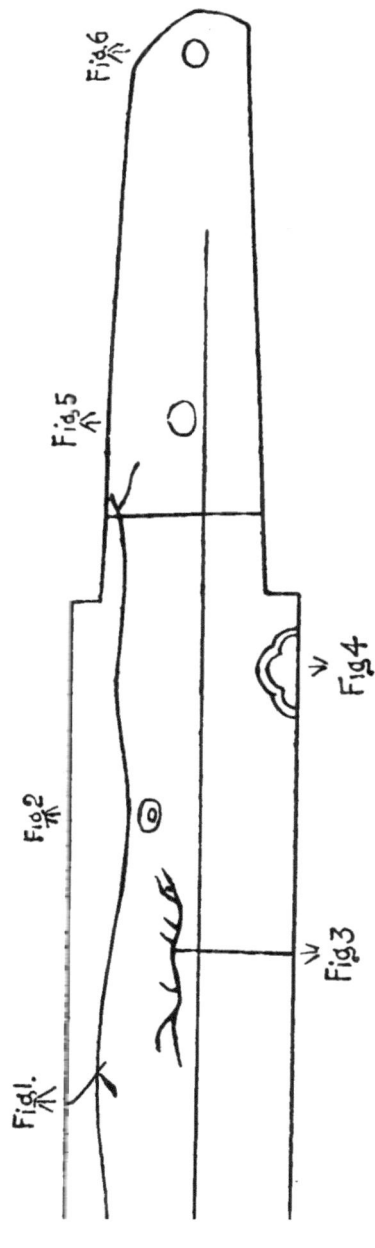

Fig.6

Fig.5

Fig.4

Fig.2

Fig.3

Fig.1.

31

PLATE III.

Figure 1. – Even if there is only one of these dots it means that one will be disowned by friends, relations and parents.

Figure 2 means an accident at sea; look out.

Figure 3 means a general commanding an army would be defeated and would die by the sword.

Figure 4. – Death will come to you soon.

Figure 5. – You will be separated from your parents.

Figure 6. – General bad fortune to the wearer.

Figure 7. – If the wearer does not become blind his wife or child will.

Figure 8. – Will never win a duel.
These are bad signs and difficult to make out. Misfortunes will happen, or you will be killed in battle.

Figure 10. – Either your wife or child or servant will meet a sudden death, or some dire calamity will happen to the owner.

Note: The descriptions to Figure 9. and Figure 11. that are shown in the drawing are also missing in the original book.

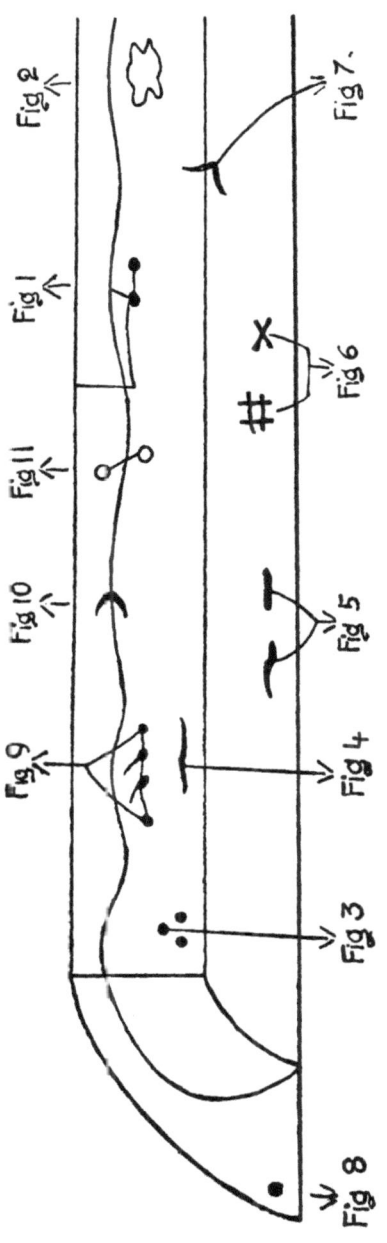

Fig 2.

Fig 1

Fig 11

Fig 10

Fig 9

Fig 3

Fig 4

Fig 5

Fig 6

Fig 7.

Fig 8

33

PLATE IV.

Figure 2. – This mark in the diagram is bad fortune and prevents attaining any social position.

Figure 3. – Thickness at the beginning of the tempered cutting edge, as diagram shows, means bad fortune; either to be killed unexpectedly, or else their home will have to be given up.

Figure 4. – Unsuccessful in everything; very probably your eyes will trouble you.

Figure 5 is a sign of general misfortune.

Figure 6 is a sign that you will be defeated, and also have no settled home. If there is only one mark it would have precisely the same effect.

Note: Figure 1. is missing in the original book; both in the drawing and in the description.

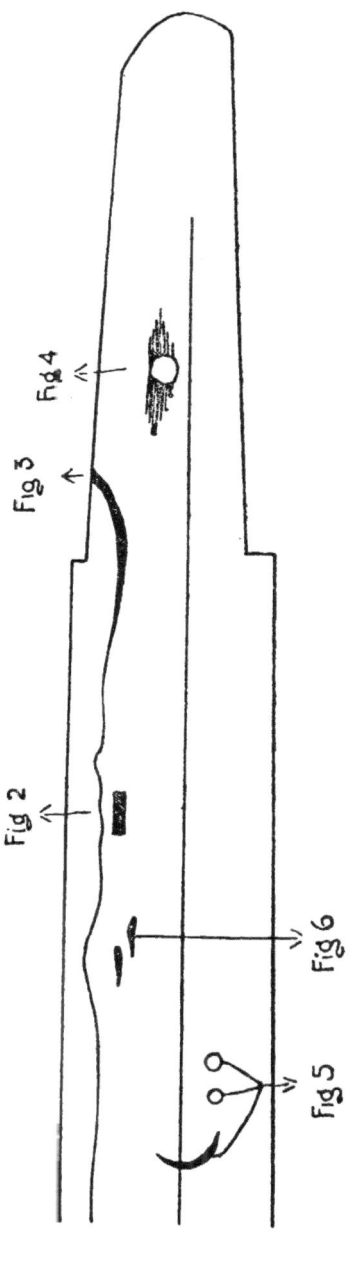

Fig 4

Fig 3

Fig 2

Fig 6

Fig 5

35

PLATE V.

Figure 1. – This mark is very difficult to detect; it means that either you will be disloyal to your master or turn traitor. Being so difficult to detect, you must practise looking at many swords.

Figure 2. – Either ill oneself or illness at home.

Figure 3. – When this mark is between the tempered cutting edge and the surface of the steel it means bad luck with children.

Figure 4. – The tempered cutting edge is sloping in this manner at the cap means you will never conquer and never raise yourself in society.

Figure 5. – Disloyalty to one's master.

Figure 6. – Worries and accidents in life.

Figure 7. – Death of your wife.

Figure 8. – Death by accident or by the sword.

Figure 9. – Others will be treacherous to the wearer of this sword.

Figure 10. – These three dots signify that if the wearer is an officer he will lose his rank, if a private person he will either lose his wife or child, or have accidents by fire or flood, or lose all his property.

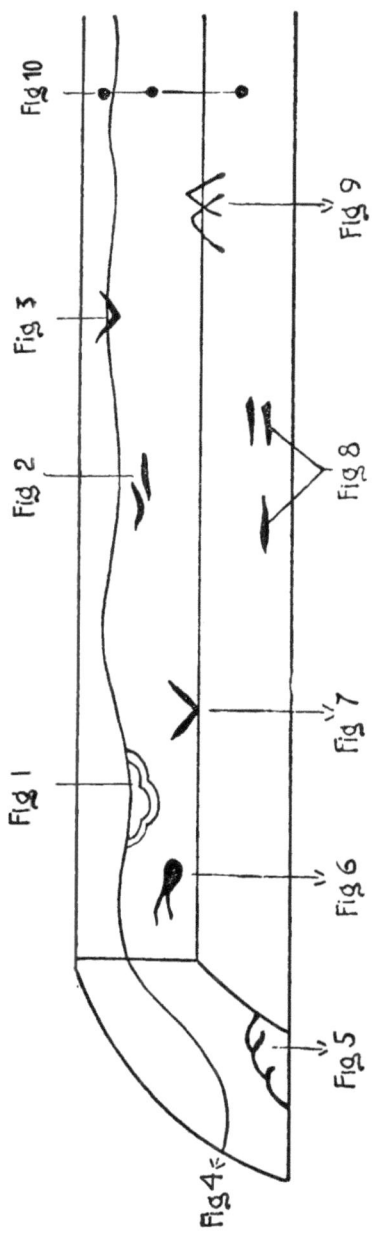

Fig 10

Fig 9

Fig 3

Fig 2

Fig 8

Fig 1

Fig 7

Fig 6

Fig 5

Fig 4

PLATE VI.

Figure 1. – These three marks mean an accident on water.

Figure 2. – Will be wronged by others.

Figure 3. – This style of ending the blade, if it is on one side only, means that the possessor is poor with low position; if it is the same on both sides it means treachery.

Figure 4. – Amibition in disobedience to one's superiors.

Figure 5. means that you will desert your commander.

Figure 6. signifies bad luck to whatever you undertake.

Figure 7. – This is a so-called dragon, and when its head points to the handle it means a disaster.

Figure 8. – These marks mean death by drowning.

Yakiotoshi means the end of the tempered cutting edge.

Note: Yakiotoshi is a katana term that refers to Figure 3 in the diagram of Plate VI. The term means that a blade's tempered cutting edge starts above the notch, delineating the blade from the tang ("hamachi"). One can find this on very ancient blades, but it more often means that a blade had its edge retempered. The latter case would make sense to associate with a bad omen.

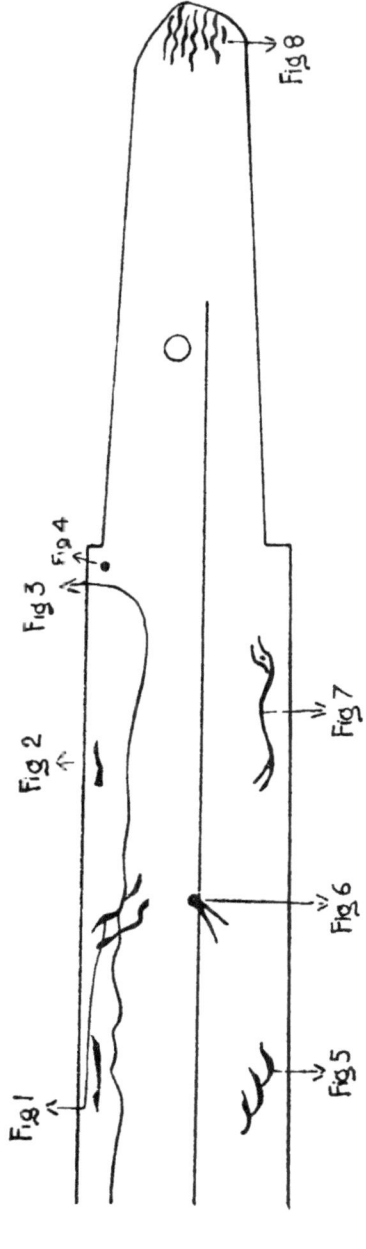

Fig 8

Fig 4

Fig 3

Fig 2

Fig 7

Fig 6

Fig 1

Fig 5

PLATE VII.

Figure 1. – An estate that has been inherited will be confiscated.

Figure 2. – Owner will be assassinated.

Figure 3. – You will be separated from your master. (Presumably means only a retainer would have a sword with marks like that on diagram.)

Figure 4. – Will have plenty of accidents by fire. (But, as the original Manuscript says, it is better to be explained by the writer.)

Figure 5. – You will be respected by no one.

Figure 6. – You will go to an enemy's country never to return. (Again original Manuscript suggests personal explanation.)

Figure 7. – A fatal accident is going to happen. So be careful, as this mark is difficult to see.

Figure 8. – Your eyes will trouble you.

Figure 9. – You will die from an accident.

Figure 10. – You will be defeated or killed by someone.

Figure 11. – There will always be disagreements between the master of the family and the members of the family and servants.

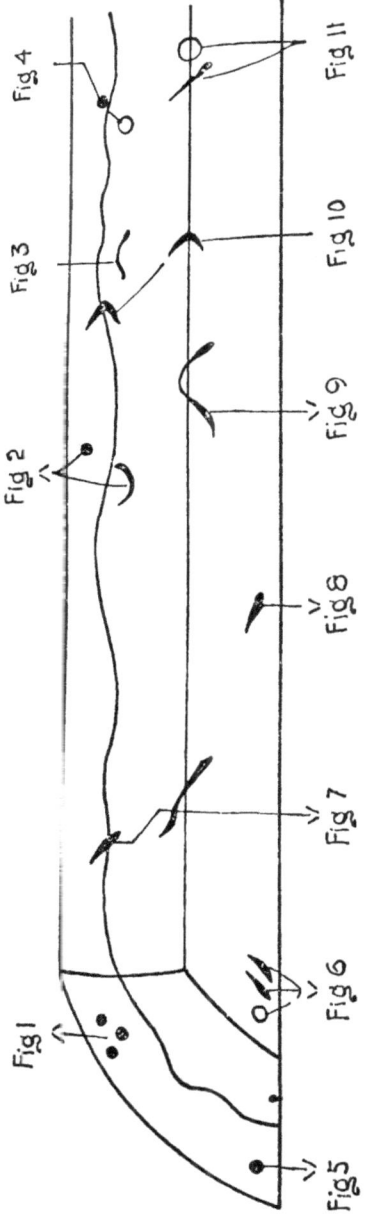

Fig 1

Fig 2

Fig 3

Fig 4

Fig 5

Fig 6

Fig 7

Fig 8

Fig 9

Fig 10

Fig 11

41

PLATE VIII.

Figure 1. – There will be frequent illness in your home.

Figure 2. – Your salary or estates will be perpetually in dispute; you will also have bad luck with your children.

Figure 3. – You will never recover from the sickness.

Figure 4. – With the tempered cutting edge running so far into the handle signifies trouble concerning a woman.

Figure 5. – Everything most unsatisfactory, and general ill-health.

Figure 6 foretells a changeable mind and many misfortunes.

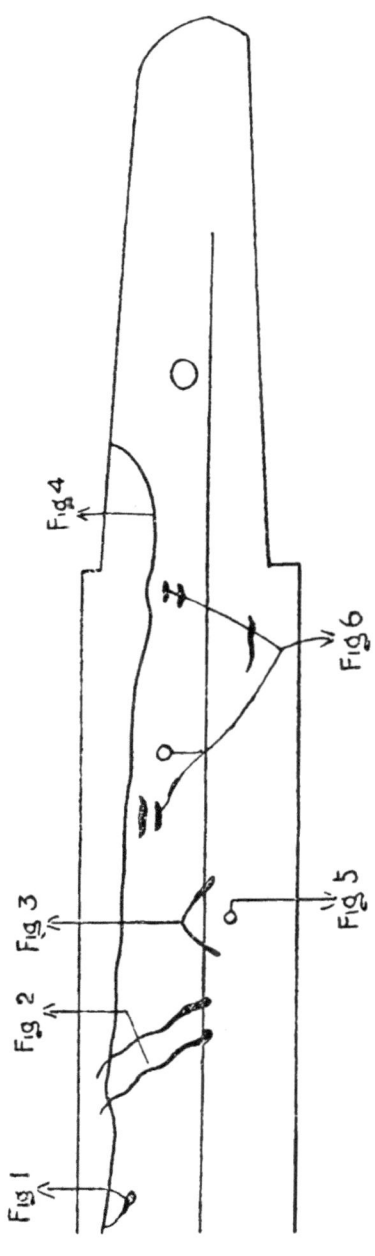

Fig 1

Fig 2

Fig 3

Fig 4

Fig 5

Fig 6

43

PLATE IX.

Figure 1. – Your health will gradually fail.

Figure 2. – This is an extremely bad sign (which can only be explained by the writer of the Manuscript).

Figure 3. – Misconduct in the family.

Figure 4. – You will lose a big case at court.

Figure 5. – The marks shown here will make the wearer excitable.

Figure 6. – An accident will happen to your eyes.

Figure 7. – A fatal accident will happen to you.

Figure 8. – This is a certain mark that the owner will commit harakiri or suicide, and even if you were to visit anybody who possessed a sword with these marks it will even then be sure to bring you bad luck; it is therefore better to break it or throw it away.

Figure 9. – You will lose your home.

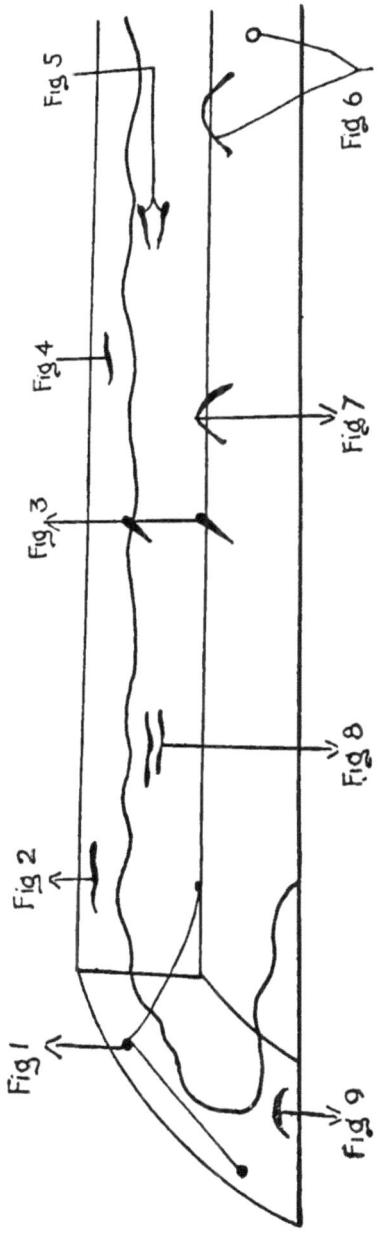

Fig 1
Fig 2
Fig 3
Fig 4
Fig 5
Fig 6
Fig 7
Fig 8
fig 9

45

PLATE X.

Hoshi or *stars*.

The writer of the old Manuscript here points out that it is in no way easy to show by writing, the destiny of the wearer of swords by their marks, and emphasises it by saying he is only pointing out marks most easily seen by beginners, and then goes on to say that this hoshi, or star, as shown in the diagram, has a ring and its centre is rather white; he likewise adds that to explain in writing is impossible, so refers you to himself.

Spirit rapping is the only means I could suggest for finding out his meaning. – J. T. C.

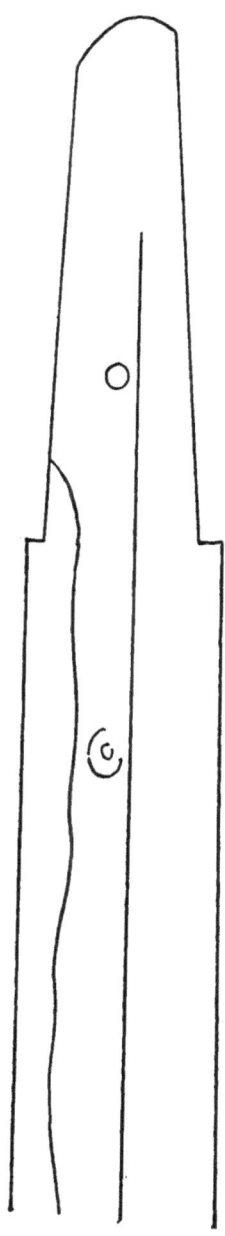

PLATE XI.

Figure 1. – The tempered cutting edge ending at the tip of the sword, as this diagram shows, signifies irritableness, and worries of the mind will never leave you.

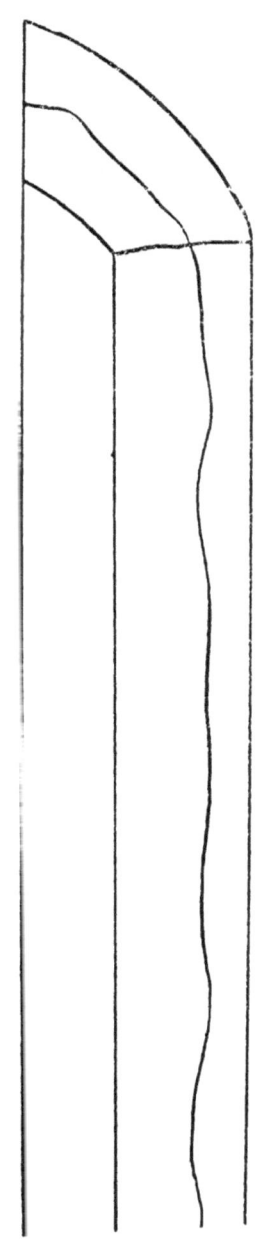

49

PLATE XII.

With the tempered cutting edge running like in this diagram and the next, points out that you will be loved by everyone, enjoy good health, prosperity in your house and family, a long life, and your social position will be greatly heightened.

51

PLATE XIII.

Shisei-saukō or *brightest of fortunes*.

This refers to previous diagram, and figure 1 shows un-failing good fortune.

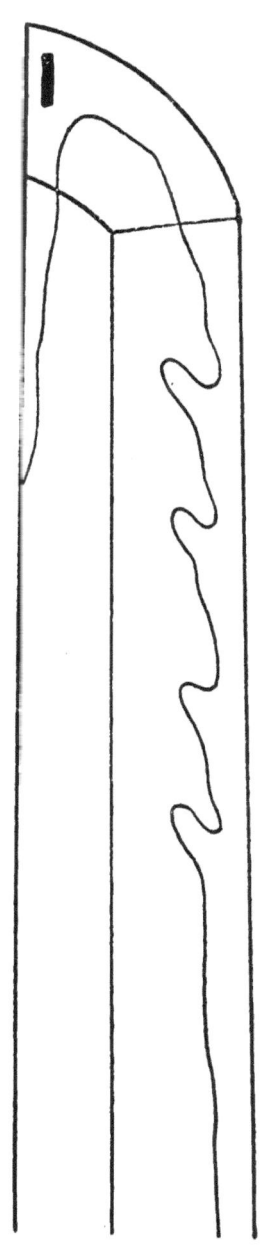

53

PLATE XIV.

Figure 1. – This is the sign of a very good sword (again the Manuscript refers you to him).

Figure 2. – This mark of a new moon signifies long life and prosperity.

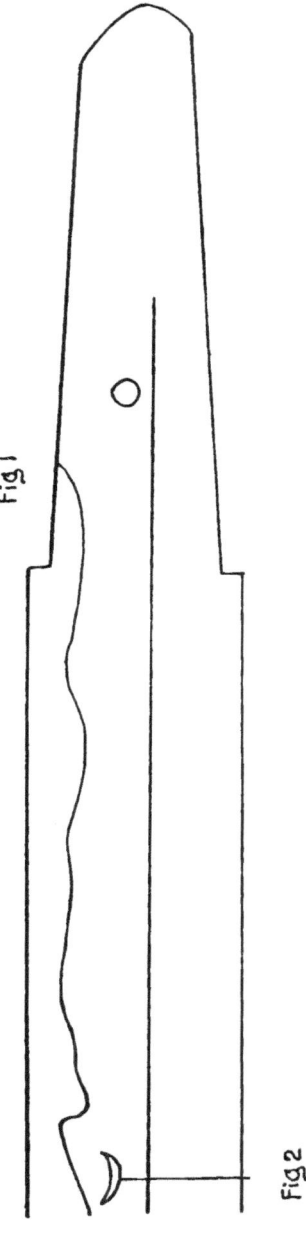

Fig 1

Fig 2

55

PLATE XV.

Figure 1 denotes that every time you fight you will be the conqueror.

Figure 2. – A moon almost in the centre of the blade and on the line is an excellent sign, signifying that luck will never desert you.

Figure 3. – This mark of a moon, especially if it is on the tempered cutting edge, signifies the height of prosperity.

Note: The description of Figure 4. in the drawing is also missing in the original book.

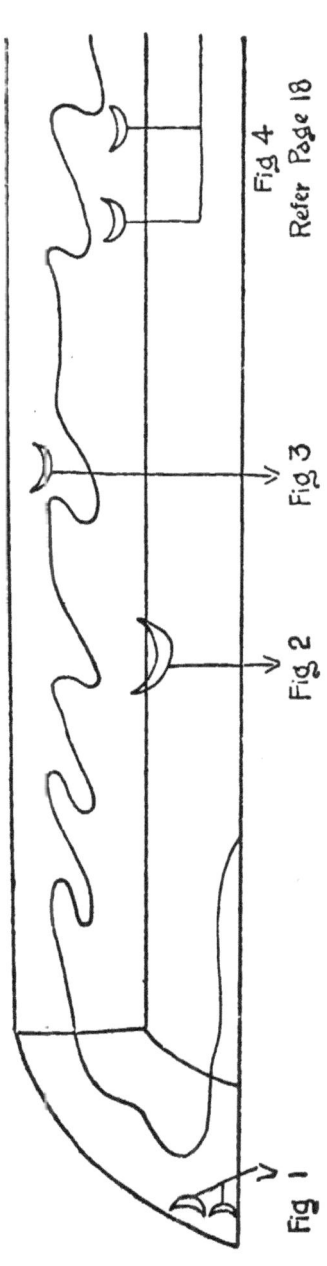

Fig 4

Refer Page 18

Fig 3

Fig 2

Fig 1

57

PLATE XVI.

Sankō, or *three lights*, denotes good fortune.

This diagram is one of great prosperity. You will live in peace, loved and respected by all.

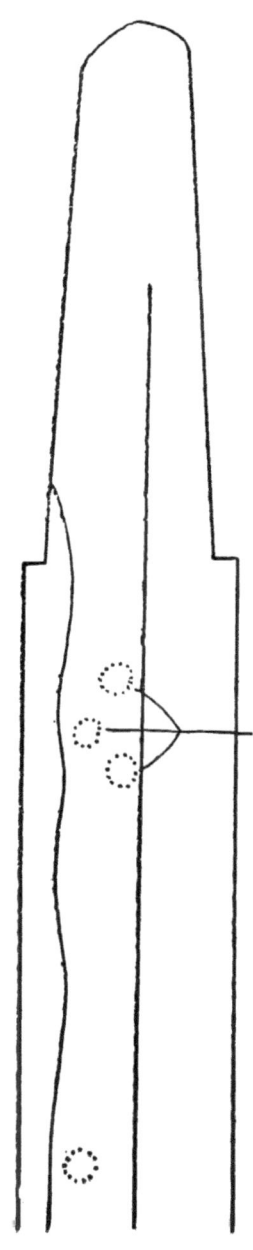

59

PLATE XVII.

Figure 1. – This is a very lucky star and unfortunately very rare.

Figure 2 represents also good fortune.

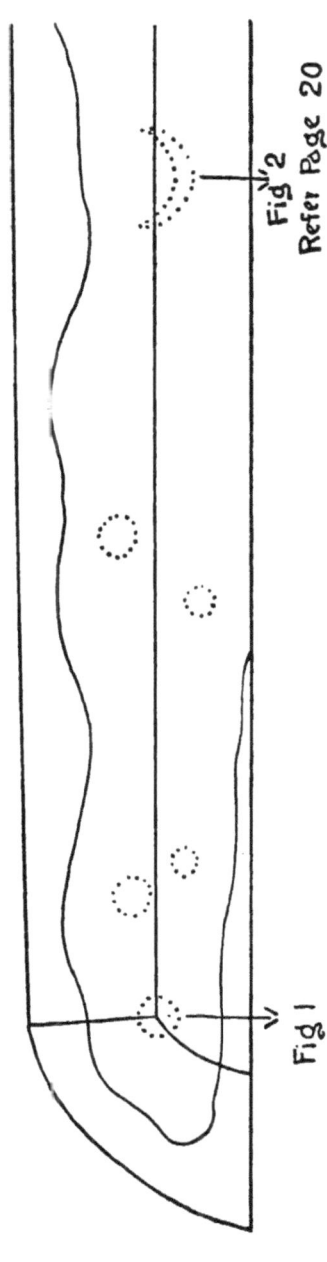

Fig 2
Refer Page 20

Fig 1

61

PLATE XVIII.

Sankō, or *three lights*.

This Sankō, or *three lights*, is considered as being very lucky.

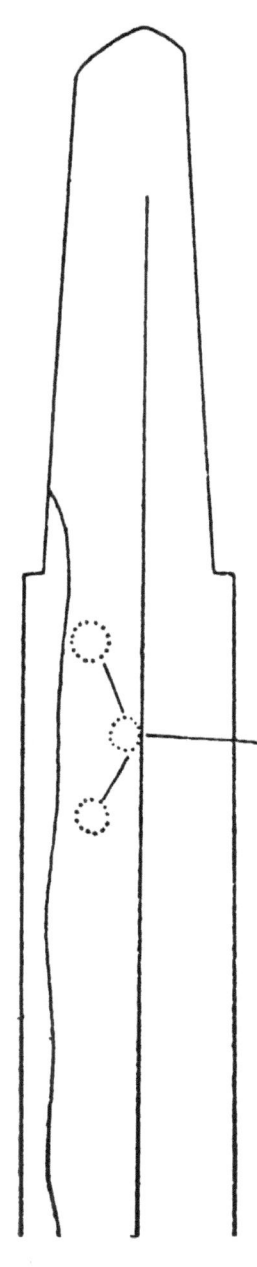

PLATE XIX.

Shichi-Sei, or *seven stars*. These seven stars are considered to represent much good fortune.

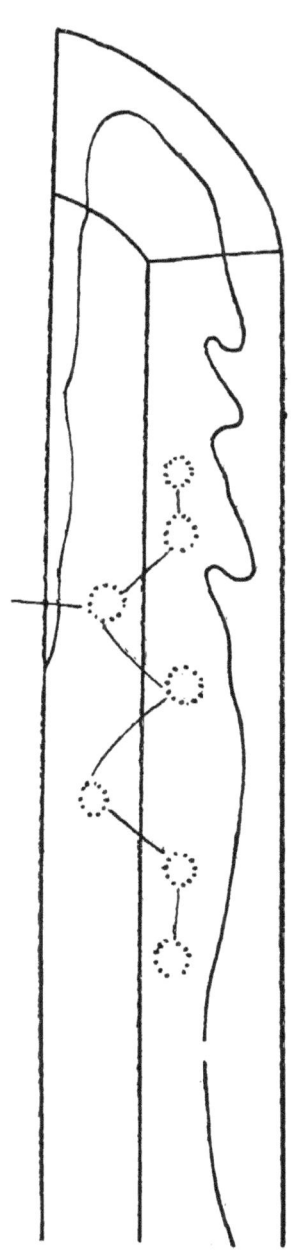

The writer of the original MSS. tells one that there are a good many people who can tell, after looking at a sword, whether it is good or not; but he seems to think that there are not many who know much about the colour or shades of swords, and which at some time or other would greatly concern the wearer's fortune or destiny. It is sad to think that so many people without knowing these facts are constantly bringing bad luck to themselves by carrying bad blades; but in order to tell fortunes by the swords it is necessary to have had many years of experience and study under an experienced master.

This is looked upon as being first class, but as they are divided into three classes it is extremely difficult to explain in writing note ancient MSS. says.

PLATE XX.

Hamon or *tempered cutting edge.*

The Hamon or *tempered cutting edge*, when fading, as the diagram shows, towards the end of the point, is not considered a very good omen. It is better to have it explained by looking at a sword.

This kind of sword tends to make you break your promises, as you are not inclined to think about what you might be saying at the time, consequently people will distrust you.

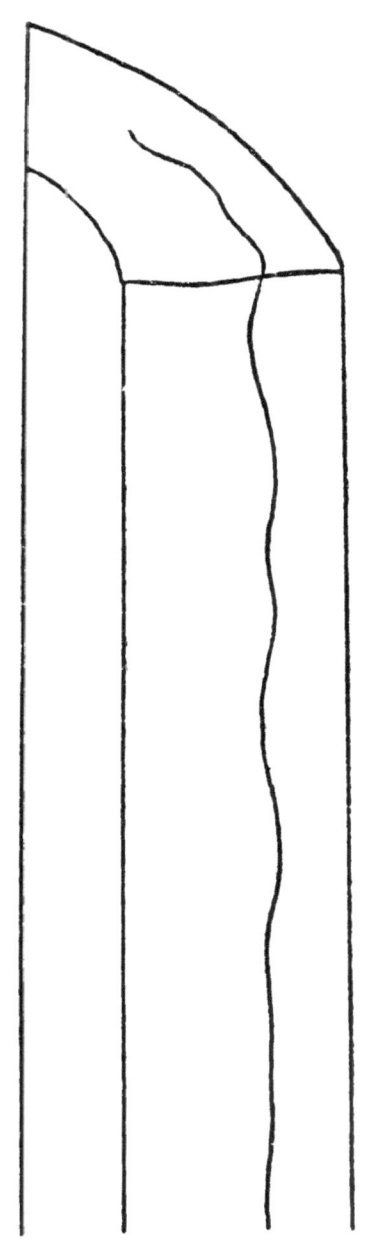

69

PLATE XXI.

Again this diagram shows the Bōshi or tempered cutting edge fading towards the end of the tip, signifying that it is a bad omen. Literally it means unsuccessfulness in everything you undertake, no determination of character, changeableness of mind and neglectfulness.

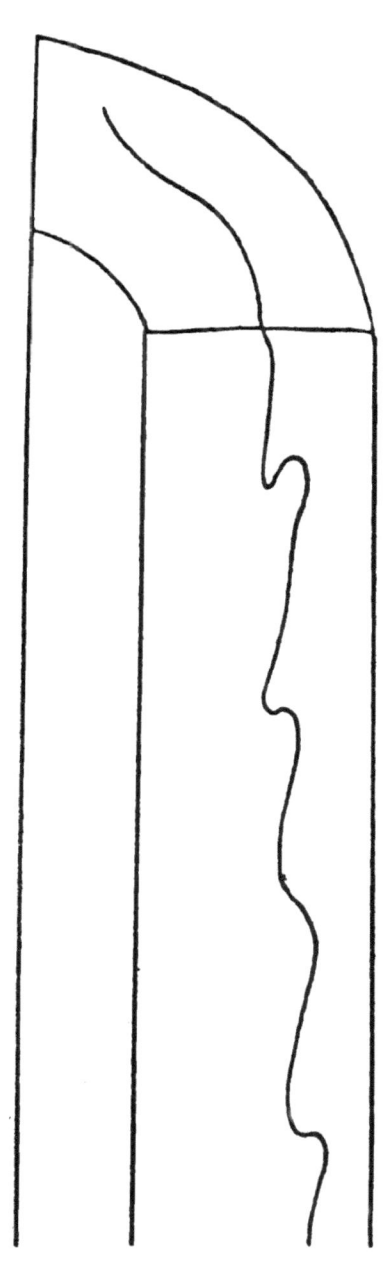

71

PLATE XXII.

Figure 1. – The Saki of either sword or dagger when cut evenly is very good luck to the wearer.

Figure 2. – When both sides of the Saki are not cut evenly it is a bad omen for the wearer.

Figure 3. – The Saki of the sword as shown in this diagram is decidedly bad luck, as it points out that the possessor will never be able to obtain a good social position.

Note: Saki generally means a point (Clifton used the word "Seki" in the original book, which, however, has no meaning in this context). In the diagram of Plate XXII., the word Saki seems to refer to the notch at the back of the blade ("munemachi") and the notch at the cutting edge of the blade ("hamachi"), where it delineates the blade from its tang ("nakago"). Yet, his references are somewhat unclear.

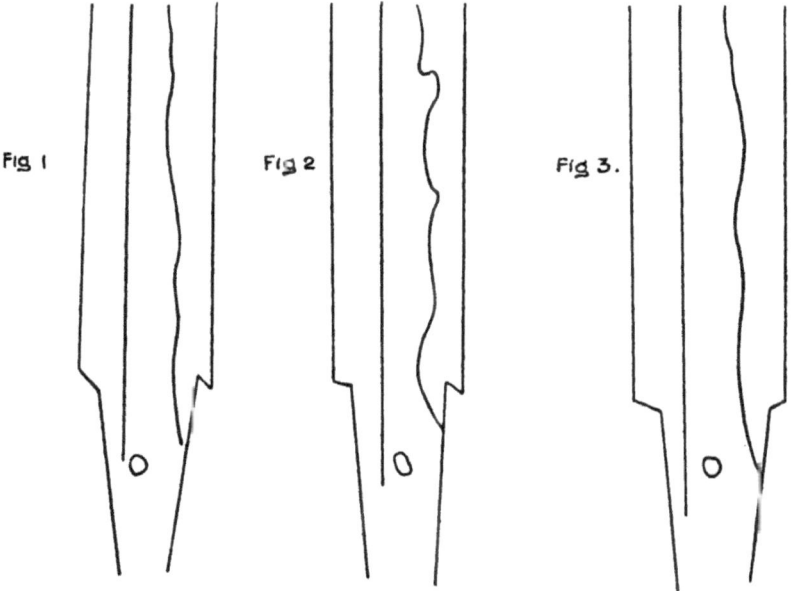

Fig 1

Fig 2

Fig 3.

73

PLATE XXIII.

Figure 1 shows that on account of the shape of the Saki that an unexpected death will occur in your family.

Figure 2. – When a Saki is cut off as the diagram shows being very shallow, bad luck will be encountered, and the owner's health will gradually fail.

Figure 3. – This diagram of the Saki fading away is again a bad sign; your health will gradually fail, or an unexpected death will occur in your family.

Note: As in the previous Plate, what Saki refers to is unclear. In this diagram XXIII. it could as much refer to how the tempered cutting edge ("hamon") ends in the tang ("nakago"), as it is drawn slightly differently between the diagrams, but so are the notches at the cutting edge ("hamachi") and at the back of the blade ("munemachi").

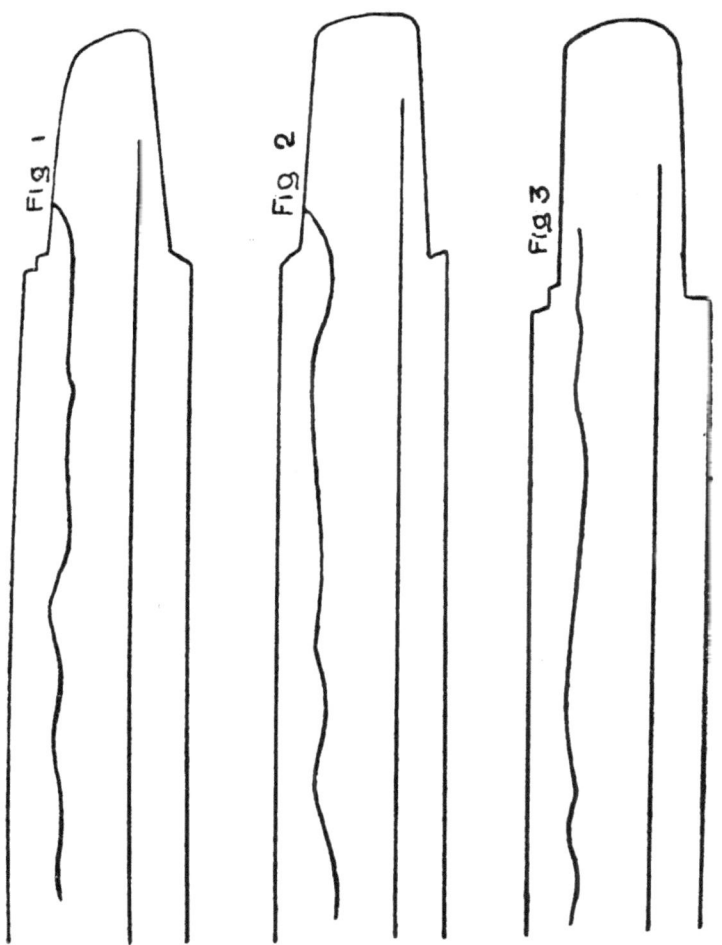

PLATE XXIV.

This deals with the figures of animals on swords.

There are too many to illustrate, but here are a few appended. The Manuscript here points out that others can be shown by looking personally at other swords.

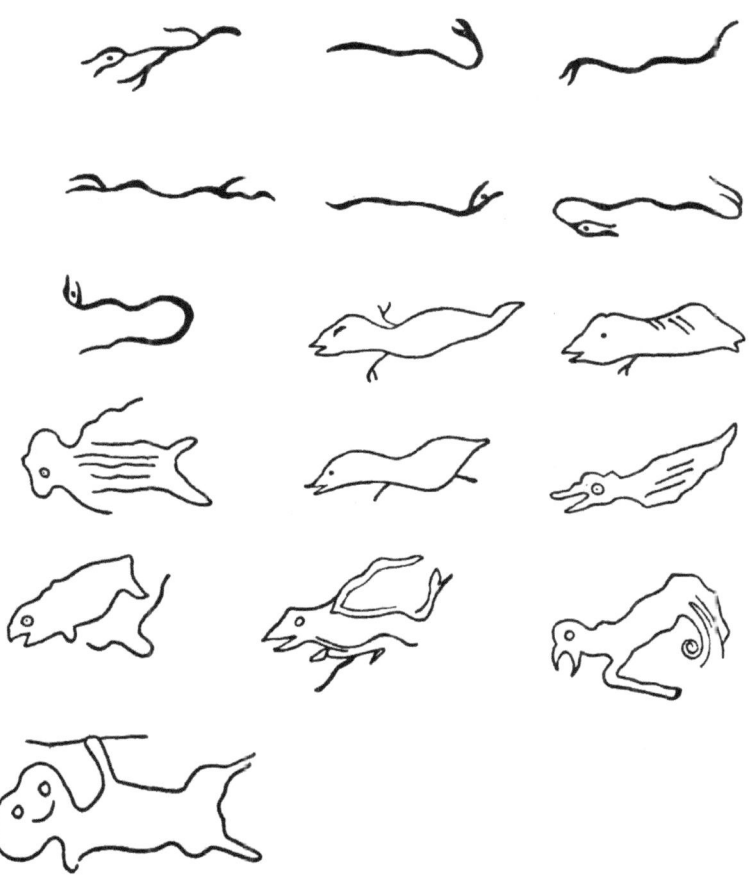

PLATE XXV.

Figures 1.

Hoshi – *a star.* Tsuki – *moon.*
Tama – *precious stones.*

These dog figures are considered to be very bad omens.

Figures 2.

These marks, which have a whitish colour and surrounded by a haze, are looked upon as extremely good fortune. You will rise in the world, but what is much more to the point you will turn out to be an excellent scholar and proficient in handwriting, but very probably you will have an excitable turn of mind.

(It would be better to explain these in person so the Manuscript points out).

Note: The reference to dog ("inu") figures comes out of context, or the diagram lacks a drawing. That a dog figure on a katana represents a bad omen makes sense. There are many Japanese words that relate to "inu" in a negative or inferior meaning. The motif of a dog is also not seen on decorative sword fittings (like menuki) for the same reason. (I know of one exception from a formal koshirae, a set of complete sword mountings, which belonged to the fifth Tokugawa Shōgun Tsunayoshi, also known as the "dog-Shōgun", born in the year of the dog. The menuki, the small metal ornament on the hilt, shows a dog on either side of the tsuka, sword handle.)

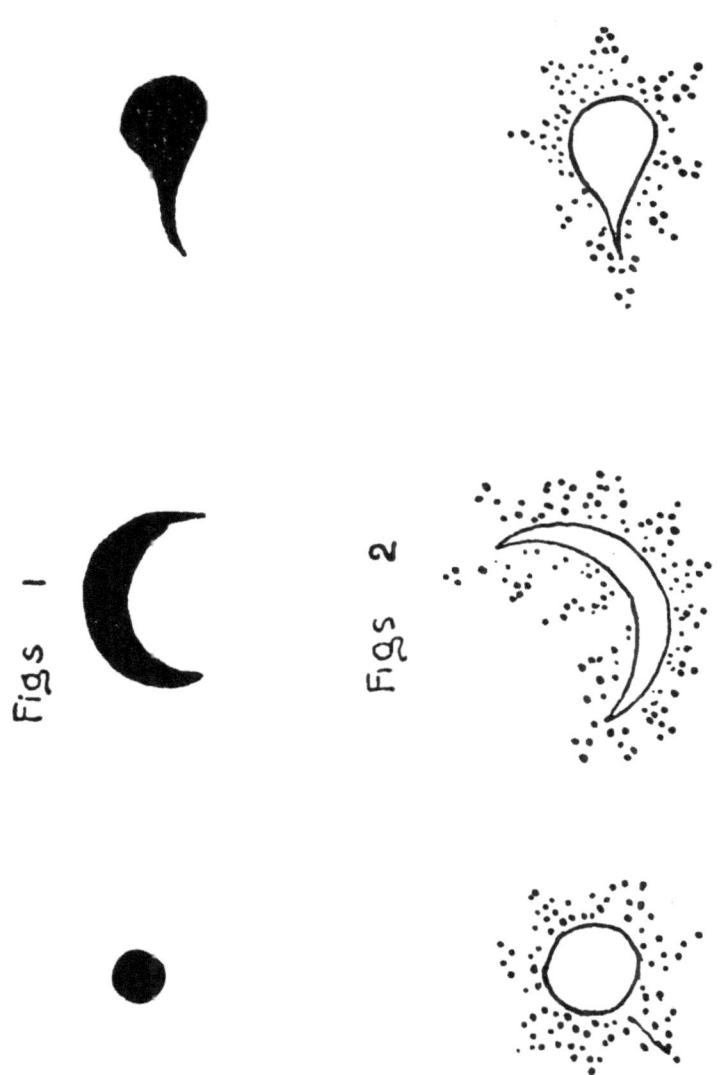

Figs 1

Figs 2

PLATE XXVI.

Kaen-bōshi. The welding of the cap being an imitation fire. To have marks of an imitation fire on the cap of the sword is looked upon as extremely bad luck, and if these marks are on both sides of blade it shows that your house will some day be burnt down, but if the Kaen-bōshi is on one side only it tends to show that one of your friends' houses will be destroyed by fire. It also represents a fiery temper, an excitable temperament, and too prone to find fault in trivial matters.

Note: The original text does not specifically refer to the Figures 1. and 2. of the drawing.

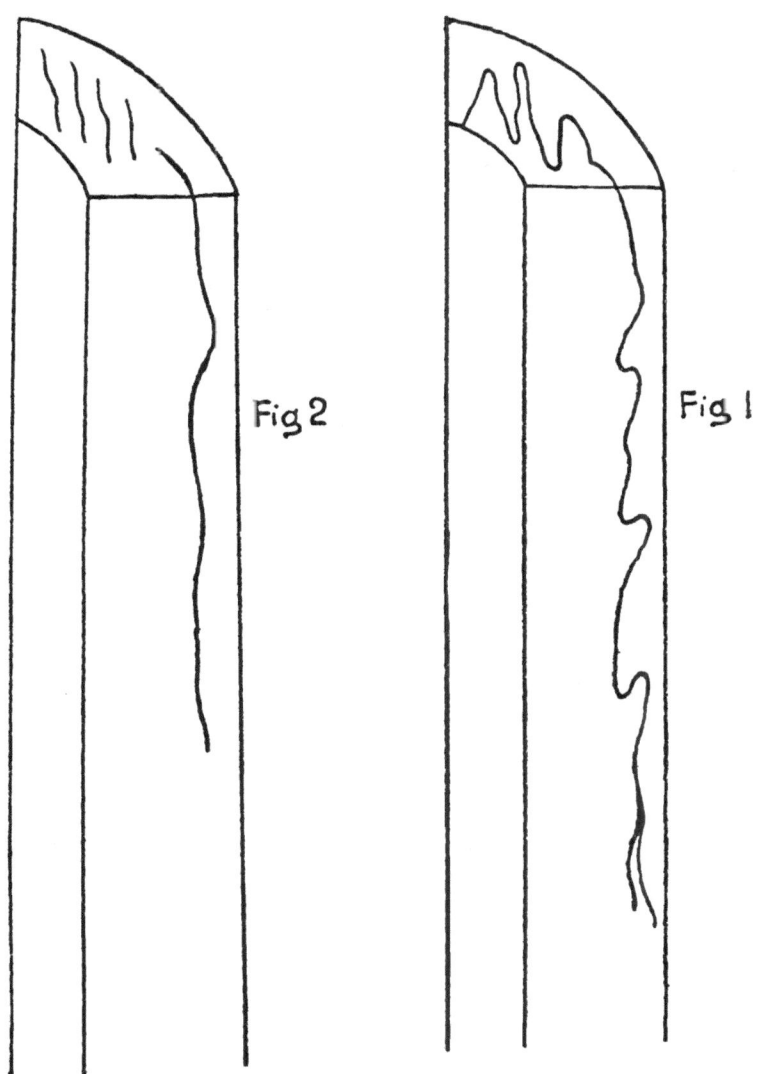

Fig 2

Fig 1

PLATE XXVII.

(Unnoba or *place of destiny*) see diagram on first page.

Figure 1. – When Hamon or tempered cutting edge ends in this fashion it is advisable not to wear this weapon, as it would soon tend to impoverish you. Likewise if the same marks happen to occur on both sides, it shows that you are a man not to be trusted.

Figure 2. – If there are any marks of this description in the Unnoba it points out that some accident or other is certain to happen to your wife or children.

Figure 3. – Whoever carries a sword with such marks as these will either die young, or contract a fatal disease.

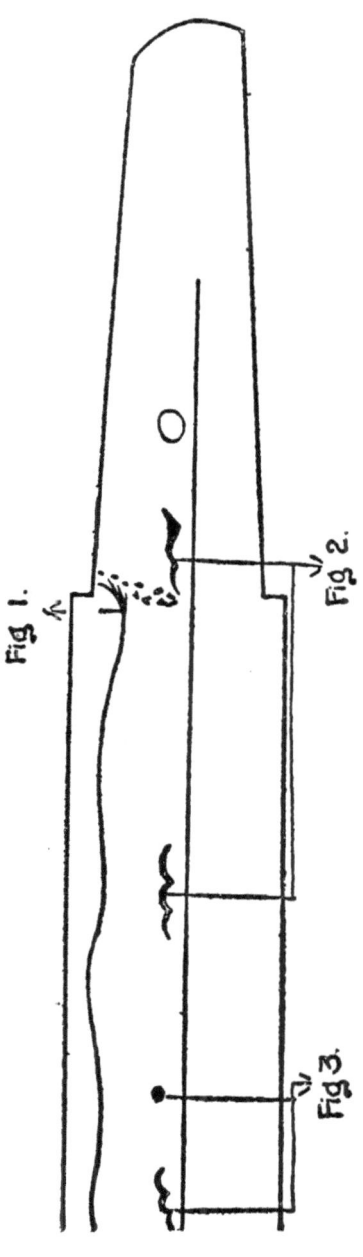

Fig 1.

Fig 2.

Fig 3.

83

PLATE XXVIII.

Figure 1. – If you wear a sword of this description you will always be in bad health.

Figure 2 points out that you will be wronged by people, and the marks will not be better for you even if there is only one ring with a black dot in the centre.

Figure 3 shows disloyalty and disobedience to your parents.

Figure 4 acknowledges a most unprincipled disposition and disloyalty to those above you.

Figure 5. – Any signs in this part of the sword are considered to be very good, moon or no moon.

Figure 6. – The owner of that sword, if he happens to be a soldier, is considered extremely lucky. His rank will greatly be raised, and he will also be respected by you.

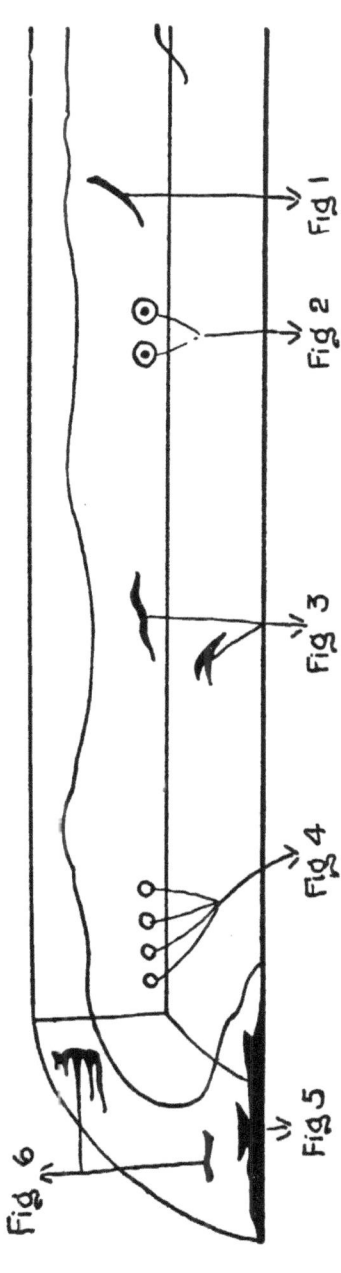

Fig 1

Fig 2

Fig 3

Fig 4

Fig 5

Fig 6

85

PLATE XXIX.

Figure 1. – This part of the sword is called Mei-life; and when the tempered cutting edge is wide at this point, as shown in the diagram, a long life is in store.

Figure 2. – If the tempered cutting edge gradually widens out from the haft, as shown in figure 2, that denotes good fortune.

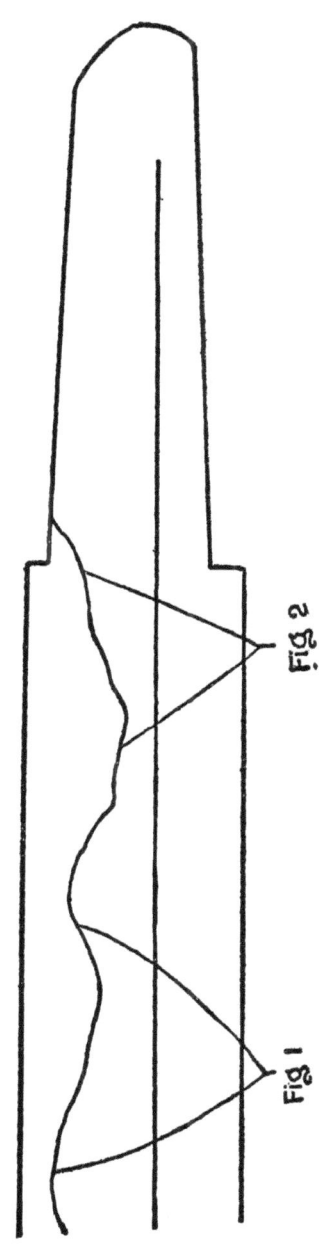

Fig 2

Fig 1

PLATE XXX.

San.   Shū.   Fuku.

Refer to diagram 1.

Figure 1. – San, or dispersing, is the point of the weapon, the tempered cutting edge well curved in, as in figure 1, is an emblem of good luck.

Figure 2. – Shū, or accumulation. If the tempered cutting edge is welded in waves you will have an accumulation of wealth.

Figure 3. – Fuku. If the tempered cutting edge at this point is narrow that also points out good fortune.

Figure 4. – Mitsugashira. This means the meeting of the three lines near the cap. Every sword possesses them.

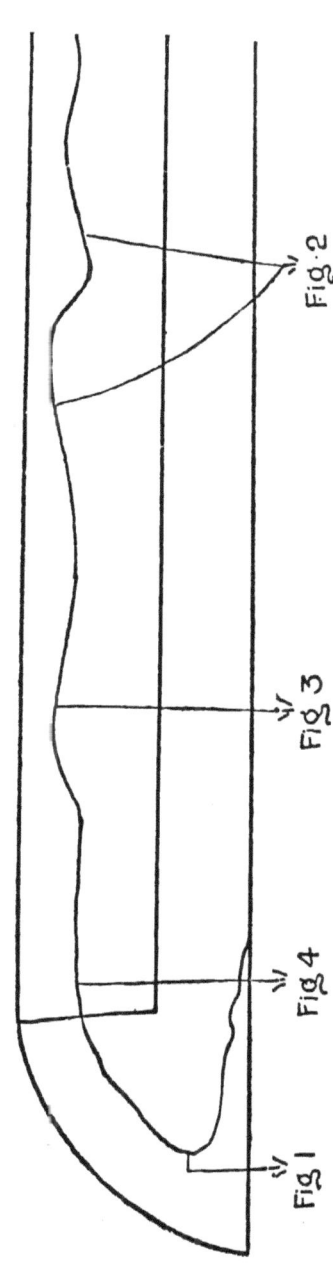

Fig. 2

Fig. 3

Fig. 4

Fig. 1

89

PLATE XXXI.

Machi is the word for the invisible line joining Saki.

The tempered cutting edge starting from the haft, as this diagram shows, is considered very unlucky; likewise, if the blade or steel part commences by being wide and perceptibly thins down, it is again considered to be a bad omen.

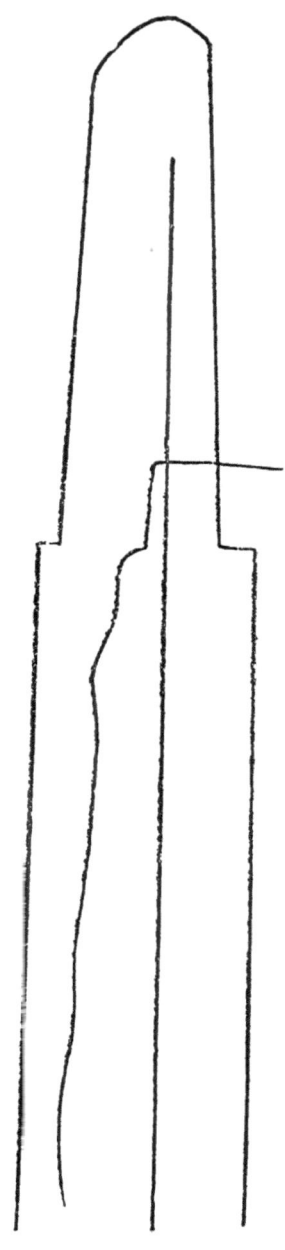

91

PLATE XXXII.

Figure 1. – The tempered cutting edge ending at the point, as shown in this diagram, is an extremely bad omen, it even goes so far as to point out that you are not even able to trust your own parents.

Figure 2. – When the tempered cutting edge at Fuku narrows that denotes good luck; but too narrow, otherwise.

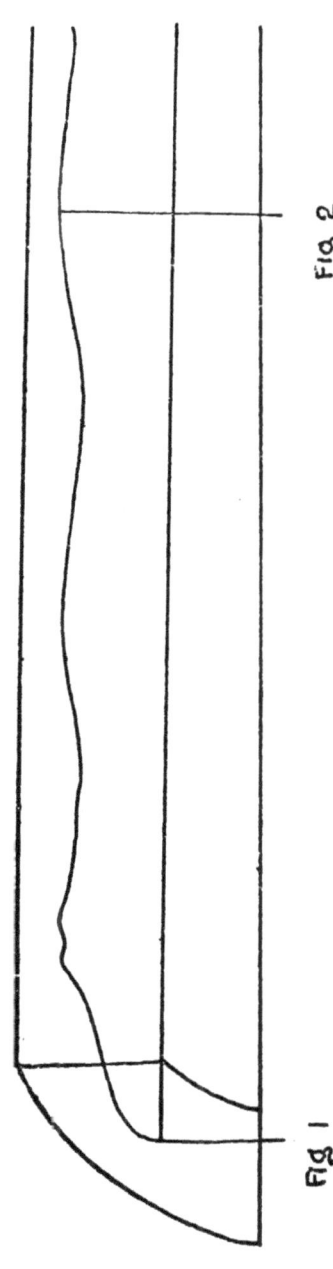

Fig 2

Fig 1

93

PLATE XXXIII.

Figure 1. – A flaw, as shown here, points out an accident, either from a horse or by water.

Figure 2. – When the tempered cutting edge begins like this you will have great good luck, but more so if it belongs to a woman; but if she does not happen to have any luck it will descend either to her husband or grandson.

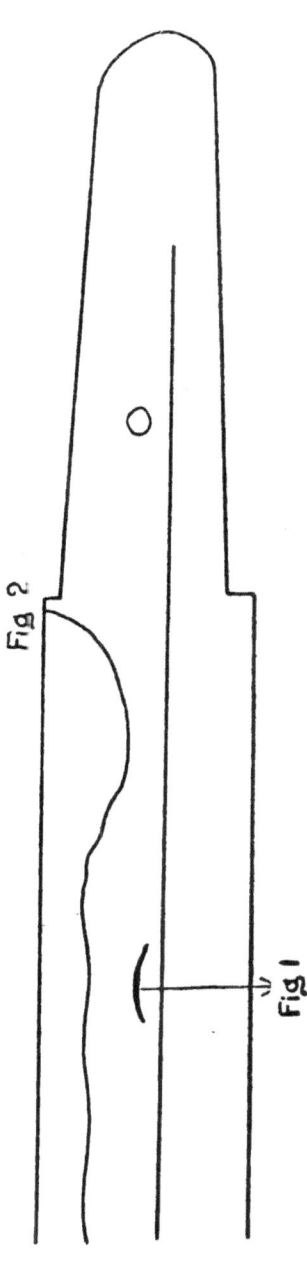

Fig 2

Fig 1

PLATE XXXIV.

Figure 1. – The figure of a moon at this point points out that you will either be killed or badly wounded in battle.

Figure 2. – A flaw in this part of the sword indicates that you will either die young or give much trouble to your parents, e.g., bad luck.

Figure 3. – A flaw in this part of the weapon, whether it is a good or bad figure, is interpreted to mean that you will be certain to lose any duel you may fight, or else that you will have an illness in connection with your eyes.

Note: The text for Figure 4. is also missing in the original.

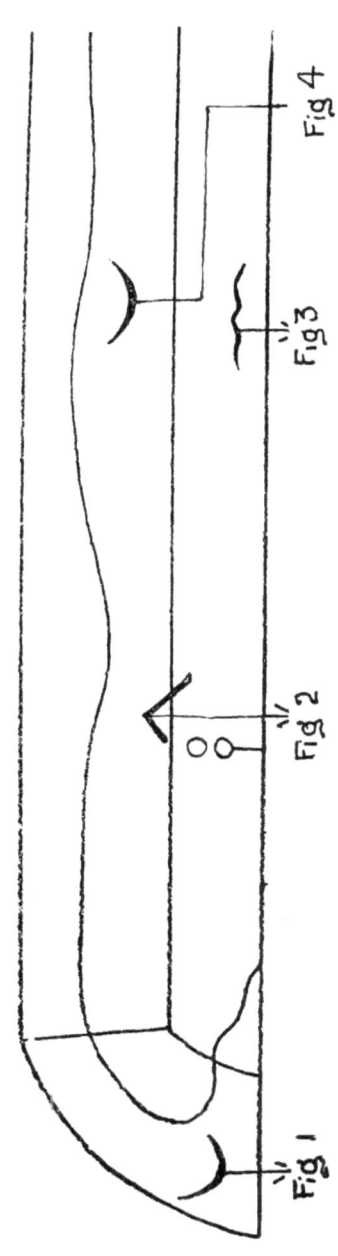

Fig 4

Fig 3

Fig 2

Fig 1

97

PLATE XXXV.

Un – *destiny.*   Mei – *life.*

The two most important parts of the sword, waves of the tempered cutting edge moving towards the cap, is a sign of good fortune.

Note: Whilst the text talks about the "two most important parts of the sword" (destiny and life) only one is mentioned and shown in the diagram on the opposite page.

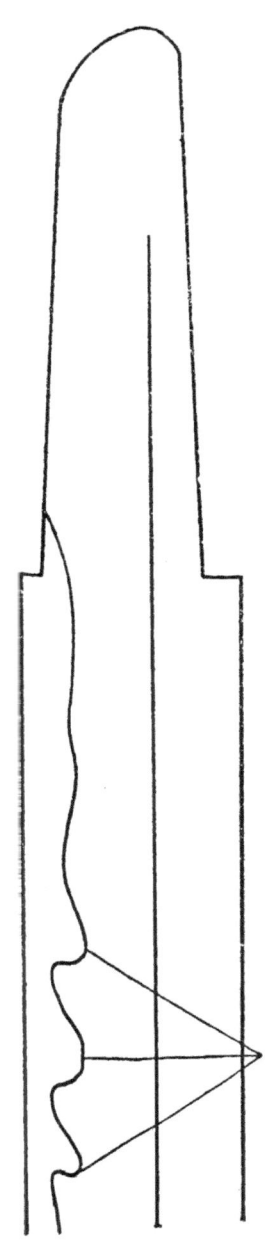

99

PLATE XXXVI.

Figure 1. – This shape of a moon, is looked upon as a portent of evil. It is called the rising and setting of the moon. (It is better to explain with a real sword, so the Manuscript says.)

Figure 2. – If there are marks on the line between Fuku and Shū it is considered bad luck. It would mean the same thing if there were marks on the line between Mei and Fuku.

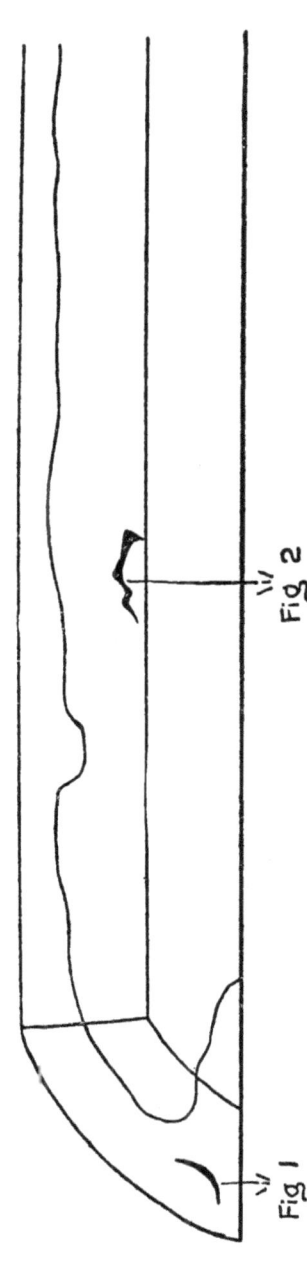

Fig 2

Fig 1

101

PLATE XXXVII.

Figure 1. – Marks of animals, as shown in this and the following diagram, are regarded as particularly lucky, but more so if they happen to be facing the enemy. (But a personal explanation is necessary, so says the ancient Manuscript.)

Figure 2. – This diagram is extremely unlucky.

Figure 3. – This is decidedly unlucky, for whatever you may undertake to do will always go wrong. Supposing the flaws are not exactly as shown in this diagram, still they would have the same meaning.

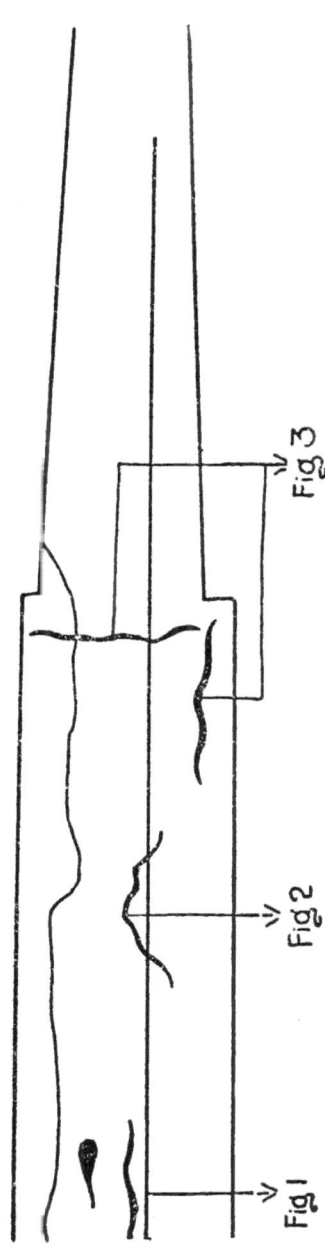

Fig 3

Fig 2

Fig I

103

PLATE XXXVIII.

This illustration of a moon on a blade is extremely lucky, and any marks of the moon on any part of the sword, if facing the point, is always lucky.

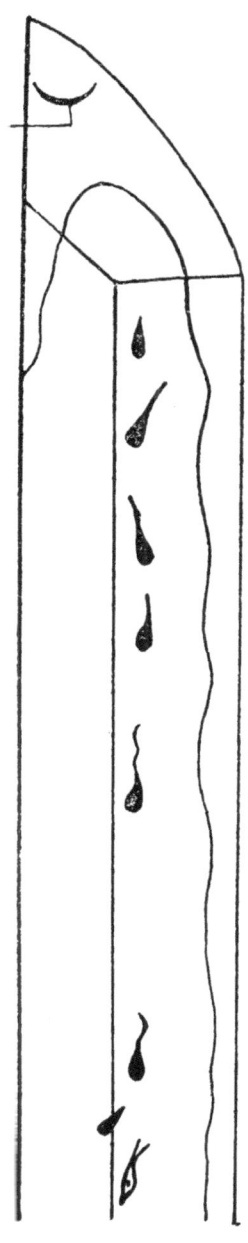

PLATE XXXIX.

Hamon – *tempered cutting edge*

Figure 1. – This is a bad flaw.

Figure 2. – Any animal moving out of the Hamon, or the tempered cutting edge, if facing or partly facing the point, is considered extremely lucky.

Figure 3. – A mark of this description, as shown in diagram, is good; but if it was in the tempered cutting edge it would be rather better.

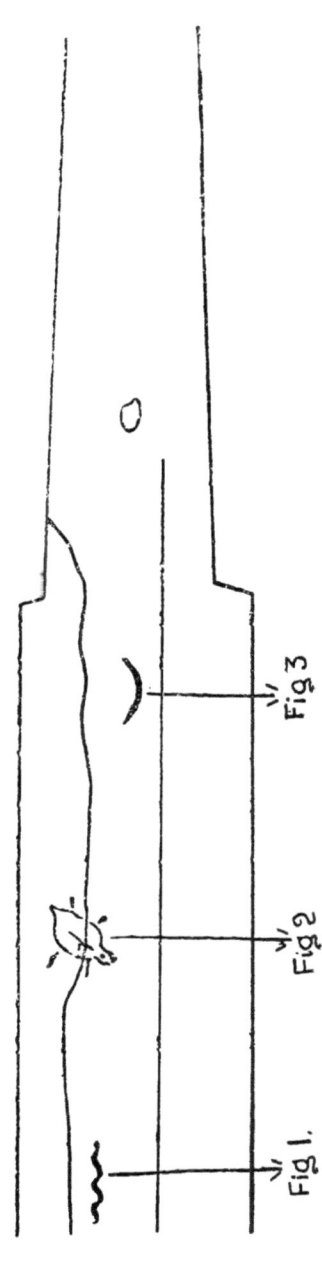

Fig 3

Fig 2

Fig 1.

PLATE XL.

Sankō, or *three lights.* Shichisei – *seven stars.*
Kuyō – *nine stars.*

Figure 1. – This has a very bad meaning and also very difficult to explain. (A personal explanation would be best, so says the ancient Manuscript.)

Figure 2. – If there are three marks of this description in the surface of the steel it is always considered excellent good fortune. They are called lights. It does not matter whether there are three, seven, or nine of these lights, they always denote good fortune, as they nullify any bad flaws the sword may otherwise possess.

Figure 3. – This diagram is extremely lucky, the animal's head being large and facing the enemy, does not matter in what part of the sword it would be in, it would always be a good omen.

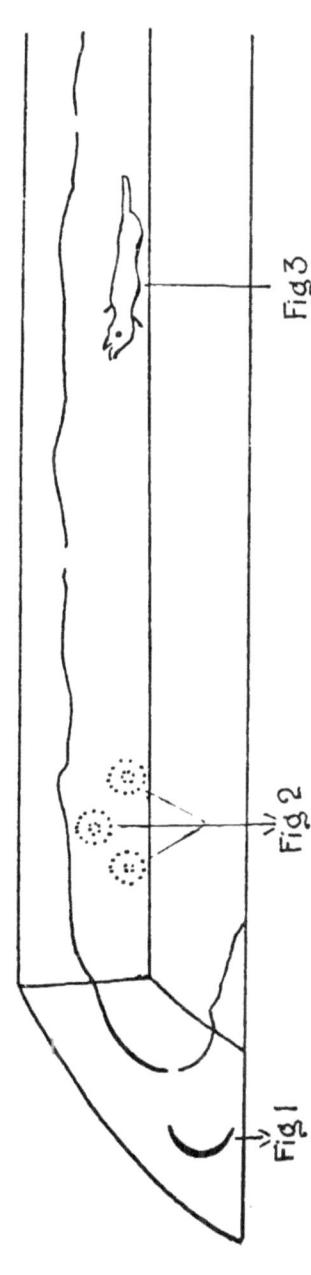

Fig 3

Fig 2

Fig 1

109

PLATE XLI.

Kissaki, or *point*.

If these flaws are in the tempered cutting edge nothing will happen, but if in the surface of the steel there is an omen of bad luck.

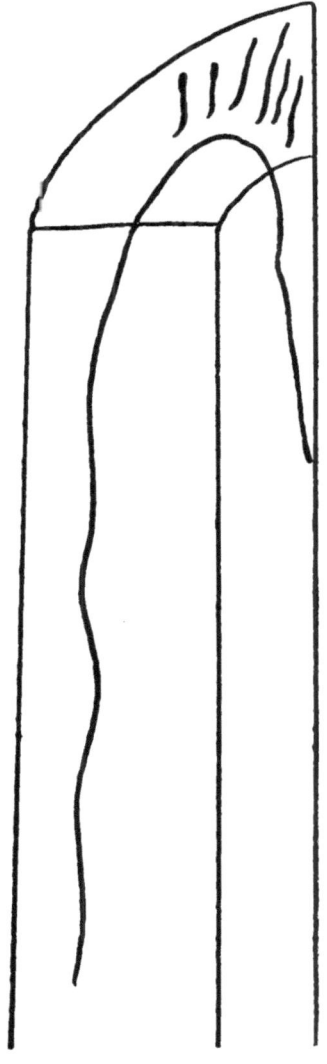

111

PLATE XLII.

Figure 1. – If some of these marks are partly touching the tempered cutting edge it is unlucky, as showing a quarrelsome nature. The author of the original Manuscript remarks that there are so many varieties of these marks he would only be able to point them out distinctively by himself.

Figure 2 denotes a quarrelsome nature and will also gain you an unenviable notoriety.

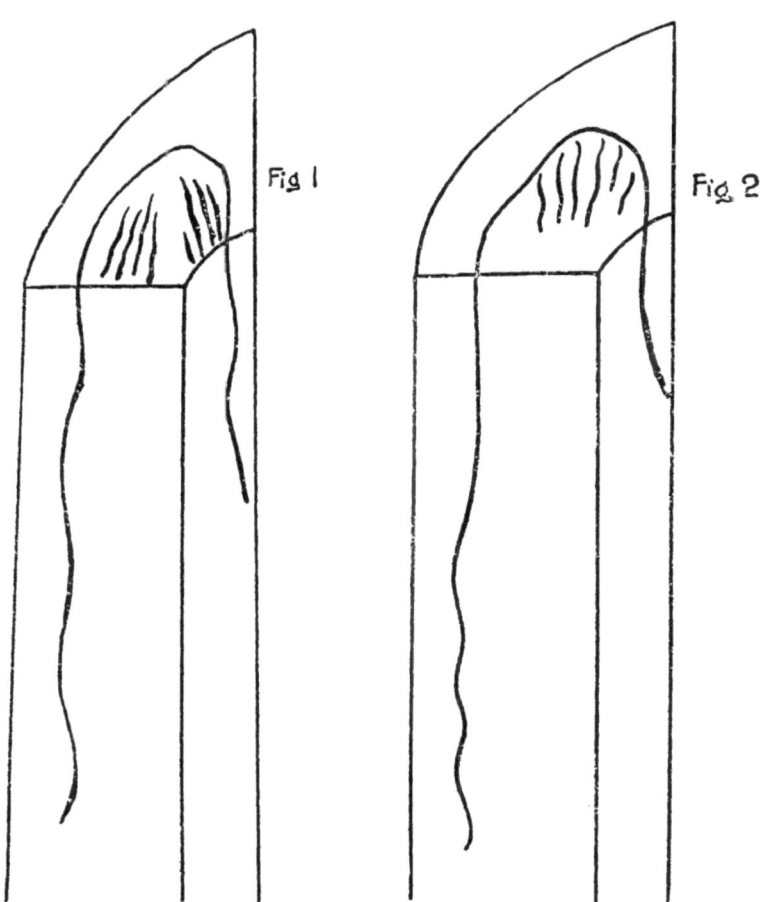

Fig 1

Fig 2

PLATE XLIII.

Figure 1. – This cross mark shows a quarrelsome disposition, and the owner would at some time or other be bound to leave his native country.

Figure 2. – This again is of no good, it would be better to throw the blade away, otherwise you will make many enemies and be often attacked.

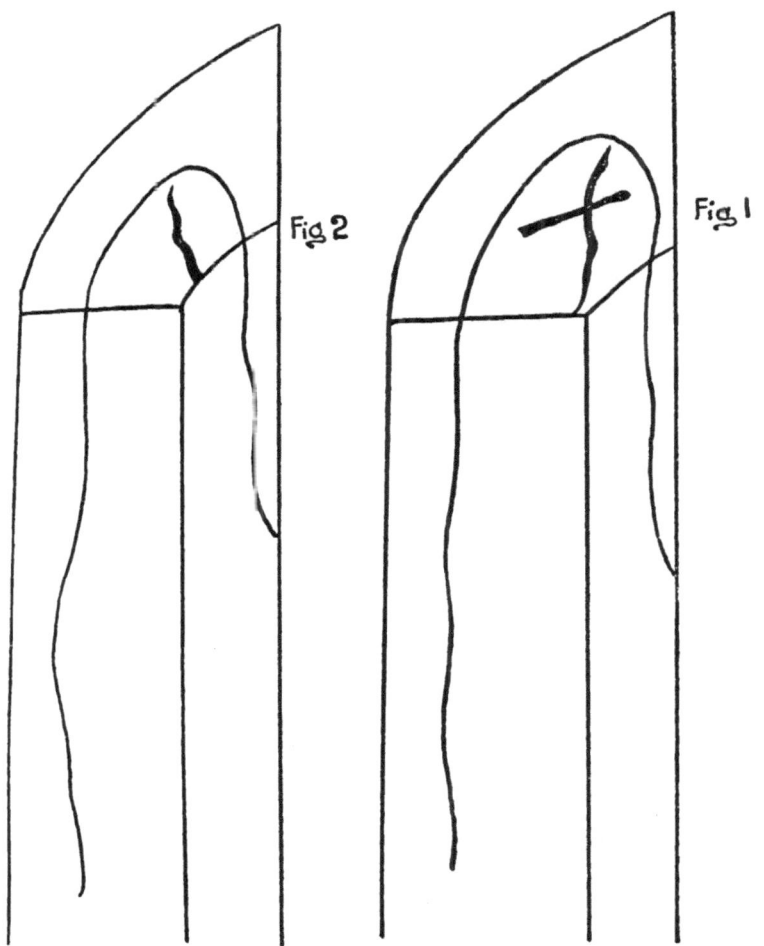

Fig 2

Fig 1

PLATE XLIV.

Yokote the straight line joining the other straight line (Shinogi).

Figure 1. – The Bōshi or cap if it bends backwards, like the diagram points out, is considered lucky, but unlucky if it is too narrow.

Figure 2. – A flaw coming out above the Yokote line is bad, certain to have trouble with winning.

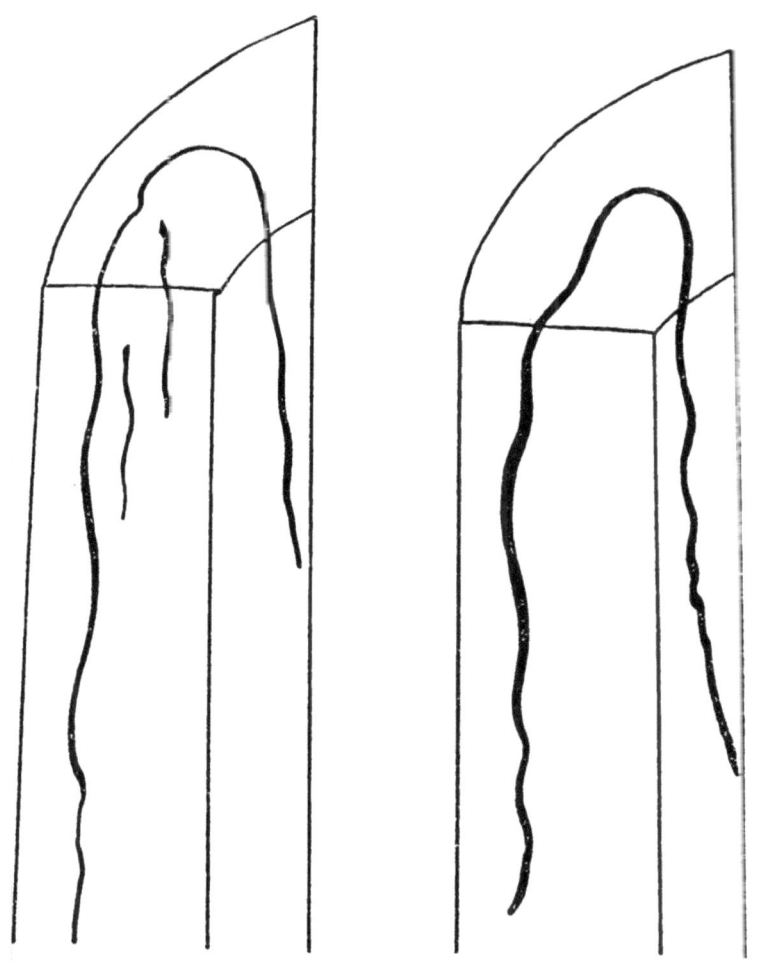

PLATE XLV.

The "Bōshi" or line where the tempered cutting edge is welded, entering the surface of the steel has many technical expressions, such as: Shimi, Hagire, Umegane, Yakigiri, Karasuguchi, Tsuki-no-Wa, Tekuirogawari.

When the Bōshi does not curve down at the cap it shows obstinacy, and that the owner will take no man's advice; it may sometimes mean conceitedness.

Note: Clifton lists here some specifically identifiable katana terms that, however, are not necessarily linked to the bōshi only: Shimi is a stain, hagire is a crack in the blade, Umegane ("fill up steel") is a cavity in the blade that is repaired by inserting steel, karasuguchi ("crow's beak") is a crack that runs inside the kissaki from the cutting edge towards the bōshi, tsuki-wa ("ring of the moon") is a crescent-shaped crack inside the cutting edge of a sword ("ha"). The word Yakigiri exists but relates to the process of making a sword (the same as "yaki-ire") but has no relation to the diagram. The word Tekuirogawari could not be identified.

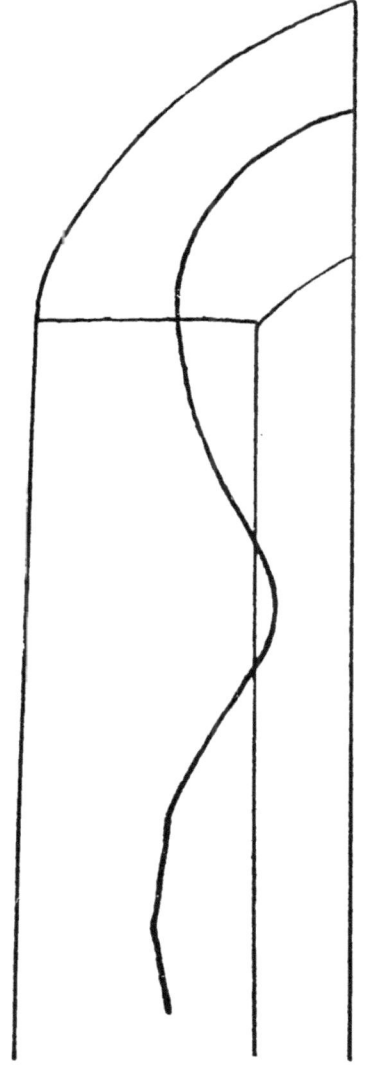

PLATE XLVI.

Figure 1. – If a sword has a mark inside the Kissaki the possessor will never attain any social distinction.

Figure 2. – When the tempered cutting edge curves up near the cap and not running to the back of the sword it denotes that you will have a slice of bad luck, either with your superior or his wife or children.

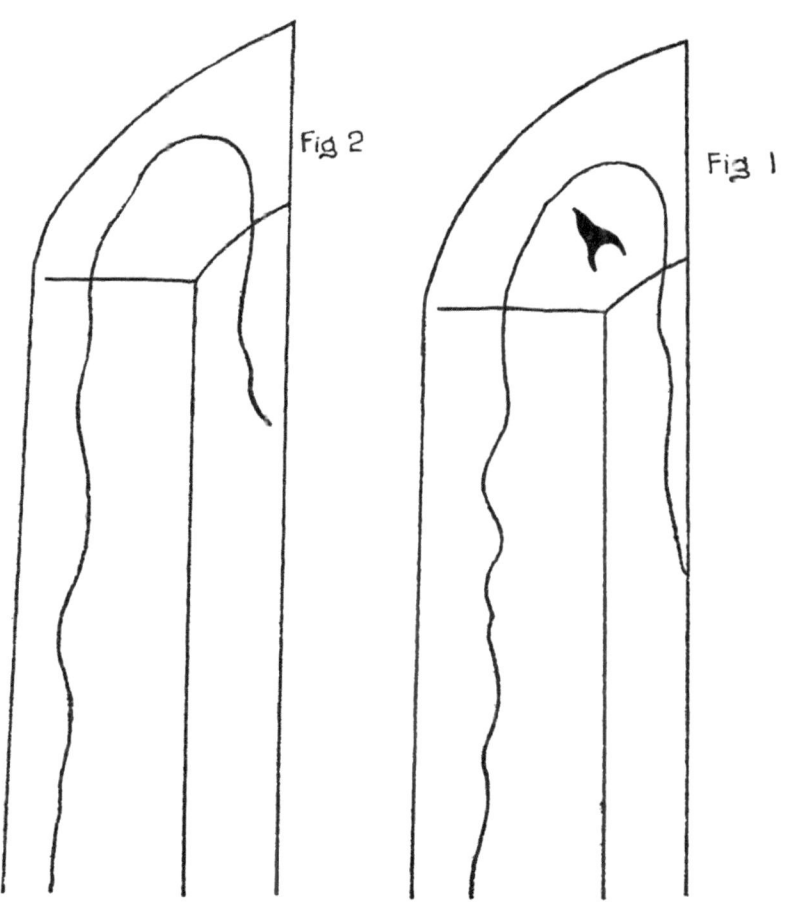

Fig 2

Fig 1

PLATE XLVII.

Figure 1. – This diagram points out the sign of meanness. It may be observed here that the back of the sword is looked upon as one's own self and the blade the enemy, therefore when the sword has a bad flaw on the back it shows that the owner of that sword is a bad and untrustworthy man.

Figure 2. – If an animal's head is turned towards the handle it usually signifies bad luck, but in this case where the animal is upside down it denotes a certain amount of good luck.

Figure 3. – Now the head of this animal is turned towards the enemy, which usually denotes good luck, but as it is bending down instead of up it points out a timid nature.

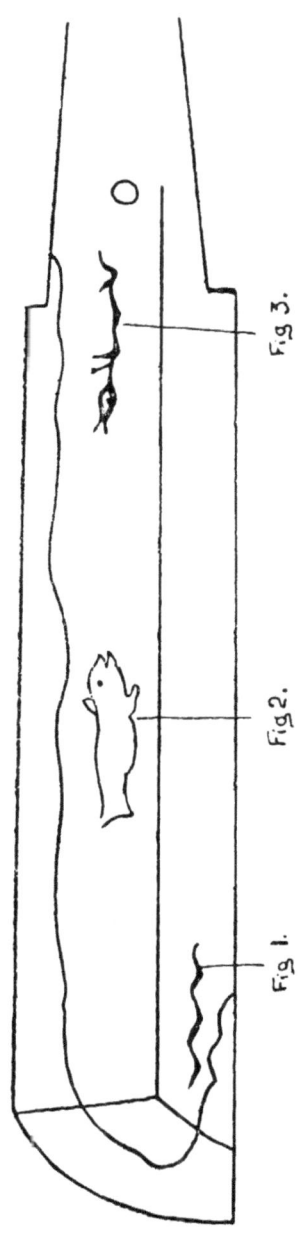

Fig 3.

Fig 2.

Fig 1.

123

PLATE XLVIII.

Shinogi or the line which runs parallel to the back of the sword.

Un– destiny.

Figure 1 is a good sign, as it is not touching the cutting edge.

Figure 2 has the same meaning as Figure 1.

Figure 3. – These marks being in the lines of Un or destiny, are bad for the owner. Luck will always be against him, and anything he attempts will turn out unsatisfactory.

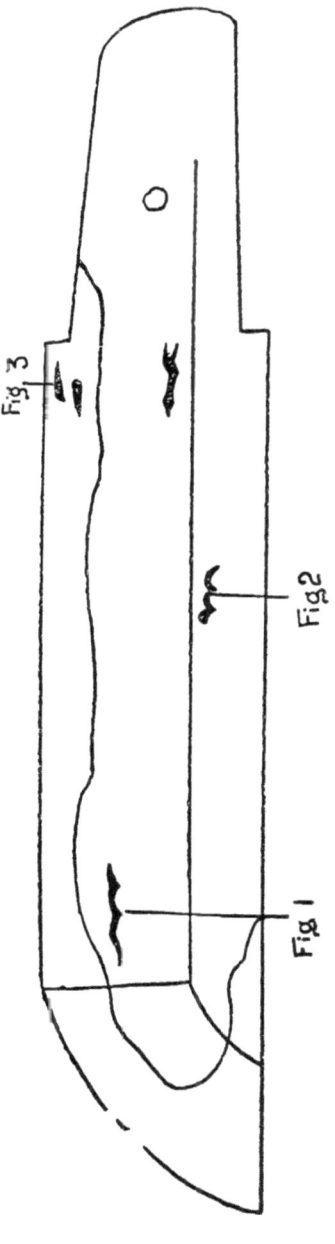

Fig 3

Fig2

Fig 1

125

PLATE XLIX.

Figure 1. – This is an excellent sign of good luck.

Figure 2. – When living things are seen in Un or destiny, it is always considered to be lucky, but in this case, where the head of the animal is turned towards its master, it denotes that the owner of the sword will turn traitor.

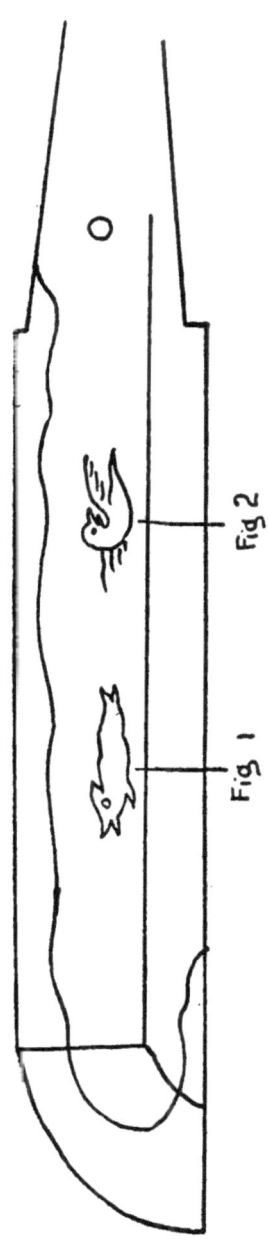

Fig 2

Fig 1

PLATE L.

An important point in reading fortunes:

Any figure of a living animal on a sword with its head turned towards the cap or point is looked upon as great good fortune in store, but if its legs are placed in an awkward position so that it appears to possess no grip, then the owner of that sword will be looked upon as a man who would hesitate, and one without sufficient energy to seize anything within his grasp, however good it might be.

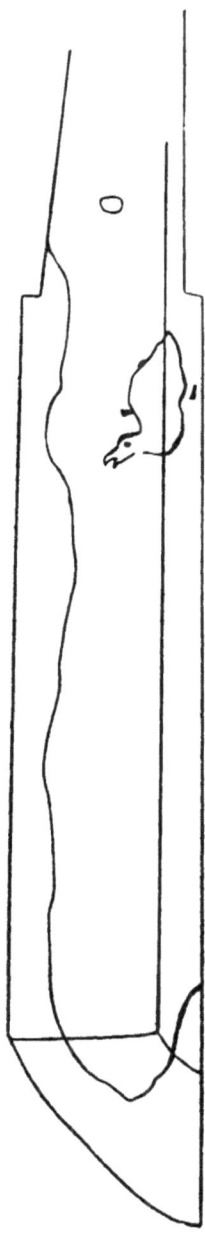

PLATE LI.

Figure 1. – This is only a second-class figure, as it seems to have faded away completely in the centre.

Figure 2. – This diagram the body is connected by a thin thread, therefore it is considered as belonging to the first class.

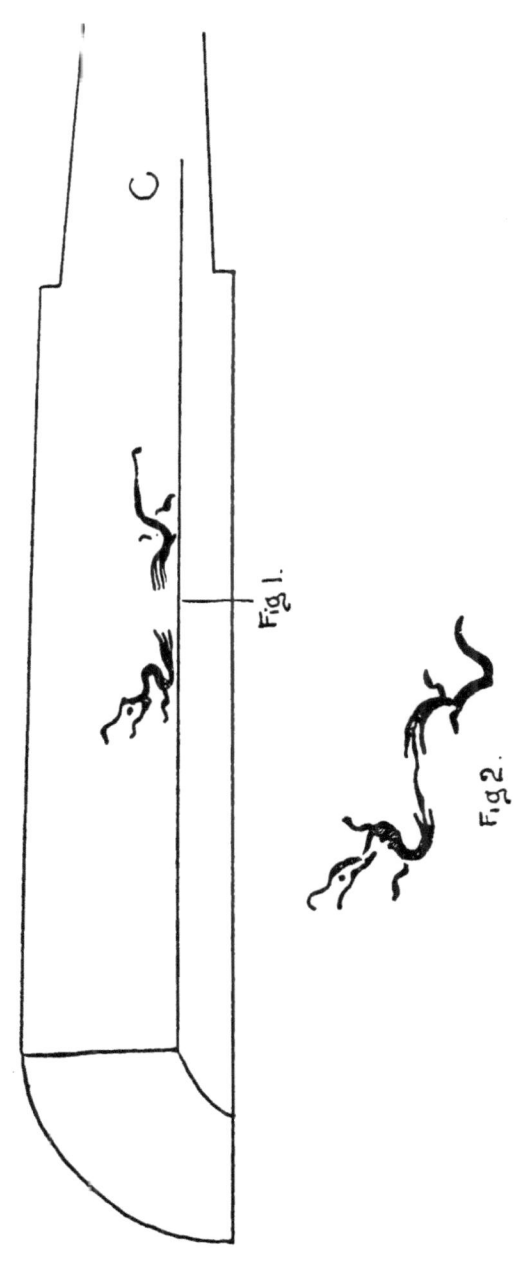

Fig I.

Fig 2.

PLATE LII.

In this figure the tail of the animal is shown to be fading away; this figure may be looked upon as being lucky, having a very good head, but as parts of it will eventually fade away it can only be placed in the third class.

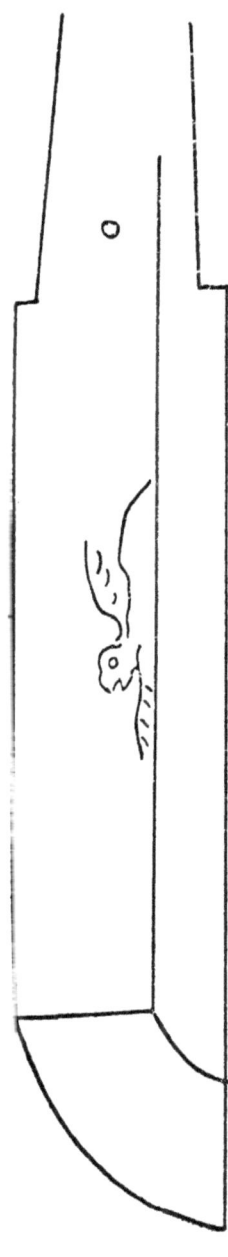

133

HOSHI or *STARS*

There are a great number of varieties of Hoshi, or *Stars*, and also a great number of different shades in the stars, by which one's fortune can be told.

The writer of the original here unfortunately goes on to say that as his teacher has forbidden him to explain any further except to professionals, he begs to be excused; and goes on to say, having been asked by a number of lovers of swords to write this book, and many hundreds of people, including the Samurai, having come to him with their sword to be interpreted, he thought it his duty to give them a general idea, so as to prevent people wearing swords that would inevitably bring them bad luck.

THE END

Corrections made to specialist katana terminology

In his book, Talbot Clifton misunderstood some words related to sword terminology. For this new reprint of "Fortune Telling by Japanese Swords", the following words were revised or adjusted to the modern spelling of a specific term:

Words used by Clifton	Corrections made for this book
Giyukurio	Gyakuryū

The Japanese word for a dragon that is upside down.

Hashi	Hoshi

The Japanese word for a star or stars.

Iron	Surface of the steel

Jigane, the visible surface of the steel of a blade.

Kasai-bōshi	Kasai-bōshi

This term was left the same. It literally translates as "fire"-*bōshi*. The drawing reflects this. However, I have not encountered such a term to describe a temper pattern *(bōshi)* in the *kissaki*.

Kitsaki   Kissaki

The Japanese term for the fan-shaped tip of a sword.

Kyuyo   Kuyō

Nine planets; arguably the most famous *kuyō* is the family crest of the Hosokawa clan.

Menuka   Mekugi ana

The Japanese word for the drilled hole *(ana)* in a *nakago*. It is for the peg *(mekugi)* to hold the *tsuka*, hilt, of the scabbard.

Mitsugabura   Mitsugashira; or mitsukadō

This Japanese term describes the point where the three lines of *yokote, shinogi* and *ko-shinogi* (the diagonal *shinogi* which continues inside the *kissaki)* meet.

Seki   Saki

The generic Japanese word for a tip. What exactly Talbot means with Seki is unclear, but he uses this term in multiple Plates, such as XXII. and XXIII. In the drawings of these two Plates', minor differences can be seen in what is called the *ha-machi* and *mune-machi*, respectively. They are the small notches on the cutting edge and the back of the blade, which separate the polished blade from the *nakago*. It looks like Clifton refers to these small notches as "Seki", or rather "Saki", tips/points.

Shimozi   Shinogi

The Japanese term for the ridge alongside a blade (on both sides) that runs in parallel to the cutting edge and goes from the *yokote* into the *nakago*.

Shioki   Shichi-ken

It is not clear what Clifton means. Likely it is the Japanese word for "seven stars sword", shichi-ken. If this is the correct interpretation, then this katana term refers to the celestial Great Bear star constellation.

Shioki sei   Shichi-sei

The Japanese word for seven stars.

Shisei sakuo

Clifton describes it as "the brightest of fortunes". It is unclear what Japanese words are meant.

Shoue   Shū

The Japanese word for accumulation.

Steel   Tempered cutting edge

Or, *ha*, the hardened cutting edge of a blade.
In this book, the "tempered cutting edge" is also synonymously used for the *hamon*, the patterned outline of the hardened zone of the cutting edge.

Umetetsu	Umegane

"Fill up steel"; a Japanese term describing a cavity in a blade that is repaired by inserting steel.

Yakie, Yaki	Hamon or bōshi, depending on context

Yaki is the Japanese word for burnt, referring to the tempered steel in a blade in Clifton's book. *Yakie* or *Yaki* has been replaced with *hamon* or *bōshi*, depending on the drawing's context, i.e., whether the words described either the tempered cutting edge along the blade *(hamon)* or in the *kissaki* only (when it is called *bōshi)*.

Yakoti	Yokote

The Japanese term for the short ridge line that runs perpendicular to the cutting edge and delineates the *kissaki*, tip, from the rest of the blade.

A short Glossary, relevant to Clifton's book
of "Fortune Telling by Japanese Swords"

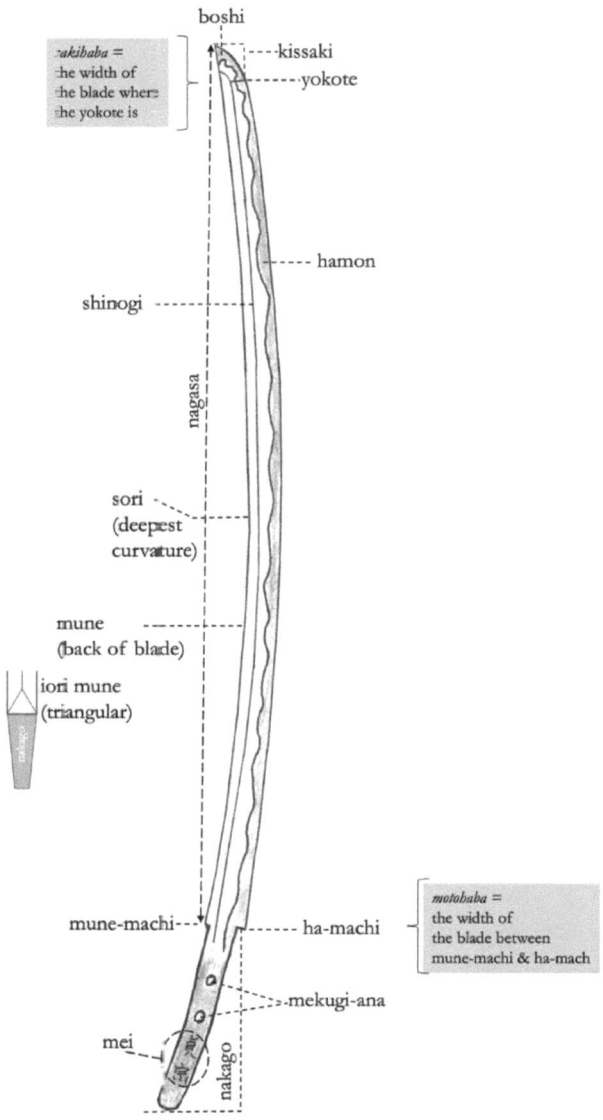

boshi

akihaba =
the width of
the blade where
the yokote is

---kissaki

----- yokote

----- hamon

shinogi -------

nagasa

sori
(deepest
curvature)

mune
(back of blade)

iori mune
(triangular)

nakago

motohaba =
the width of
the blade between
mune-machi & ha-mach

mune-machi---

---- ha-machi

---- mekugi-ana

mei

nakago

bōshi 帽子
Patterns of the *hamon* in the *kissaki*, resulting from the heat treatment following the clay coating on the blade surface. Basically, it is the *hamon* in the *kissaki*.

chōji midare 丁子乱れ
Chōji is a clove-shaped pattern; elements of the *hamon* that resemble cloves with a roundish upper part and a narrower lower part. There are different types of *chōji*, such as *chōji midare*, an irregular clove pattern.

hamon 刃文
The blade pattern produced through the heat treatment of the blade that involves the clay coating. The *hamon* outlines the transition between the region of harder steel with martensite at the edge of the blade and the softer steel with pearlite at the centre of the blade.

jihada 地肌
The visible pattern of the forging structure in a blade, or the grain.

kissaki 鋒
The tip of the blade, measured from the yokote to the very hardened tip of a sword. There are different types of *kissaki*.

mekugi ana 目釘穴
Describes a hole in the *nakago* (and in the *tsuka*) to insert a peg (the *mekugi)* which is usually made of bamboo.

nakago 茎
The tang of a blade; the part that is inside the hilt and not visible. Usually the *nakago* has one hole, to fix the hilt onto the sword with a peg. A blade can have one or several holes. The signature of the smith and other information (such as a date or nickname) was carved into the *nakago*.

nie and *nioi* (Example of a *notare hamon*).

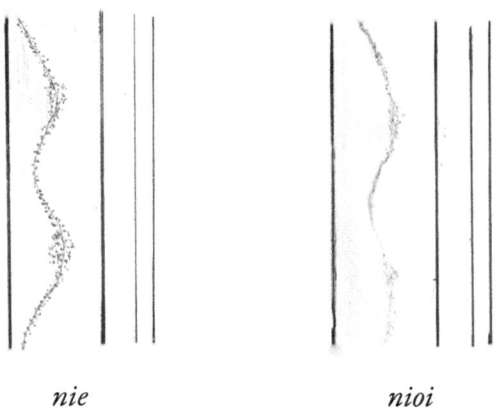

nie   nioi

Nie are martensite crystals visible to the naked eye. *Nioi* are much smaller crystals that are no longer individually recognizable to the eye and therefore merge into a ribbon. An accumulation of *nioi* is therefore often compared to the Milky Way.

nihontō 日本刀
Literally "Japanese sword". The word is a generic term describing all types of Japanese blades.

tobiyaki 飛焼

Literally flying burnt elements. Roundish martensite formations in the *ji* that are not connected with the *hamon*.

tsuka 柄

The handle of the sword. The *tsuka* has a hole that overlays the *mekugi* ana in the *nakago*. A wooden peg, usually made of bamboo, was inserted to fix the handle onto the tang.

Sources

Clifton Mary Violet, "The Book of Talbot", Wildside Press, 2011

Kapp, Leon and Hiroko, Yoshindo Yoshihara, "The Craft of the Japanese Sword", Kodansha International, 1987

Kennedy, John, "The Clifton Chronicle – The Story of a Great Lancashire Family", Carnegie Publishing Ltd, 1990

Nakamura Keisuke 中村圭佑, 刀箱師の日本刀ブログ ("Katana Case-Maker Blog"), essay entry of 3rd July 2021, title: 刀の吉凶を占う「剣相」(Katana no kikkyō wo uranau kensō – "Fortune Telling with Katana"); https://note.com/katana_case_shi/n/n639c8eea7a96

Rogers, Graham, "Lancashire landowners and the great agricultural depression", Northern History, XXII, 1996, pages 250-68

Sesko, Markus, "Legends and Stories around the Japanese Sword", Vol. 2, Lulu Enterprise, Inc., 2012

ABOUT DANIEL BÜRGIN

Daniel Bürgin, born 1963 in Lenzburg (Switzerland), moved 1993 to Tokyo, where he still lives. He has published several books in German: "Kwannon" (Short stories from Japan), 2006. "On the Search of Yamato" (Essays), 2009. "The Devil's Oak" (a fairy tale), 2010, illustrated by Peter Säuberli. "Tokyo-Fukushima Journal, March/April 2011", 2012. "Muteki —➤ without Enemy" (Stories about Japanese swordsmiths and swords), 2020. "The assumed grave of Masamune" (Essay), 2021. "With a Pure Heart – Terao Naomasa, Samurai of the early 17th Century, and his Katana" (2023 in German and English).